THE GREAT AMERICAN

Text by
Jeff Fair

Photography and Technical Editing by
Lynn Rogers

Box 1360, Minocqua, WI 54548

Once believed to be a semi-human link with the animal world, the black bear's human-like form and actions still evoke feelings of kinship. The black bear, the only living bear that evolved in North America, is truly the Great American Bear.
Front cover photograph: Lynn Rogers.

This book is dedicated to the memory of Patch, who contributed a powerful volume of information toward our understanding of black bears, and who died in the Boundary Waters Wilderness this autumn, the object of an age-old proposition between man and bear.

Printed in Singapore.

Designed by Origins Design, Inc.

NorthWord Press, Inc.
Box 1360
Minocqua, WI 54548

For a Free Catalog describing NorthWord's line of nature books and gifts, call 1-800-336-5666.

Library of Congress Cataloging-in-Publication Data

Fair, Jeff.
    The great American bear / text by Jeff Fair ; photography and
technical editing by Lynn Rogers.
        p.   cm.
    ISBN 1-55971-079-9 : $ 39.00
    1. Black bear.   I. Rogers, Lynn L.   II. Title.
    QL737.C27F35   1990
    599.74'446--dc20
                                                    90-7974
                                                    CIP

C O N T E N T S

"Never get between a mother and her cubs."
"A bear can take your head off with a single swipe."
"Not all bears are Yogi and Gentle Ben."
"A bear gives no warning before it attacks."
"Don't go into the woods. There are bears in there."

These are the warnings I grew up with. Everything I read and heard portrayed wild bears as brooding, hungry, and short-tempered. Books and magazines told and retold of killings, noting little distinction between black bears and grizzlies. I discovered from my childhood pets (snapping turtles, snakes, and such) that wildlife danger is often exaggerated, but I had no experience to help me understand bears.

My experience with bears began twenty-three years ago, in 1967, when I started working with black bears as a student aide for the Michigan Department of Natural Resources. On my first day, when my boss told me that a treed bear had descended and run right past him, I couldn't imagine a threatened bear coming that close without attacking. I knew there had been bear incidents in national parks. I knew people had even been killed, and I was apprehensive.

My apprehension soon turned into fascina-tion. I moved to Minnesota in 1968 to begin a black bear study that became my life work. I studied bears as a profession and photographed them in my off-time. Part of the fascination was the power of the bear. Bears charged or lunged at me. Bears I thought were drugged in dens sometimes turned out to be inhospitable. Bears in culvert traps slapped at the peepholes when I looked in. I thought I was having close calls and I remained cautious. But over the years I realized that not one of the hundreds of "close calls" had ended in contact. Charging bears always stopped, even when I was capturing their squawling cubs. Threatening bears always ran when I jumped at them or threw rocks. Furious bears in culvert traps became suddenly timid when I opened the door for them to escape, exiting only when they saw an escape route that was clear of people. Inhospitable bears that startled me in dens did not bite, seeming content with my undignified retreats. I became convinced that the black bear is characterized much more by restraint than by ferocity.

I still wondered about the killings by black bears (twenty-five reported across North America this century, as of this writing) until I put them in perspective. I learned from the National Center for Health Statistics that for every human death from a black bear in North America there were approximately the following numbers of deaths from other causes: seventeen from spiders, twenty-five from snakebite, sixty-seven from dogs, one hundred fifty from tornados, one hundred eighty from bees and hornets, and three hundred seventy-four from lightning. For each death from a black bear, there are over 90,000 homicides. I began to feel safer in the forest than in the city, and bears became the least of my worries. Lightning, tornados, and bees are far greater threats.

I also stopped worrying about being cuffed or bitten, even though I knew people have been scratched or nipped while crowding around panhandling black bears to feed or pet them. I knew by then that bears sometimes treat bad-mannered people the same as they do bad-mannered bears and that the resulting injuries, if any, are usually slight, due to black bears' restraint. Outright attacks are almost as rare as the killings. For example, in the Boundary Waters Canoe Area Wilderness where I worked, people had spent over a million visitor-days per year, for decades, camping among the seven hundred or so bears of the area with only two attacks, both by the same bear. No campers were attacked while hazing hundreds of wayward bears out of their camps over the years. The more aggressive the people were, the more the bears retreated.

When I realized how minor the threat actually is from black bears, a new research door was opened for me—trying to study them up close like Dian Fossey did gorillas. To my surprise, black bears were more accepting of a person than I had imagined possible. At first the bears were as apprehensive of me as I initially had been of them. They expressed their discomfort with the usual lunges and bluff-threats that black bears do under those situations. I still jumped back when bears bluffed particularly convincingly at close range. Eventually, we both developed a comfort and trust that allowed the bears to go about their peaceful activities and me to expand my attention beyond the bears themselves. Soon I was walking through the woods, day or night, watching bears forage, play, rest, and mate just a few feet away. (Males that joined estrous females were the quickest to ignore the inconsequential human.)

Technician Greg Wilker joined the North Central Forest Experiment Station research team, and together we fine-tuned methods for a formal study. Soon we and others were walking and resting with the bears for twenty-four hours at a time, recording the bears' every bite and action as they foraged, napped, nursed their cubs, and slept through the night. Suddenly, the bears were providing information I could only wonder about in my previous studies—everything from how they communicate to what forest types they seek for each seasonal need. The information is helping forest managers preserve the best bear habitat and is helping campers deal more knowledgeably with bears. The study is continuing with a new set of technician trainees each year, and I am still spending my non-study hours photographing bears across the country to illustrate the findings.

Biologist-author Jeff Fair spent several weeks with the study bears, our data files, and us. He visited bear researchers across the continent. He used his firsthand knowledge and broad perspective to good advantage in this insightful, authoritative book. I like his clever ability to weave so much solid information on the life, struggles, and disposition of the black bears into a perceptive picture of the bear's place in North America today. His chapter on Greg Wilker's day with the bear provides the best insight into a bear's daily life I've ever read. This is a book that finally gives a fair and balanced portrayal of the Great American bear.

My thanks as well to Mary Olson, who did the research for the Foreword.

Lynn Rogers
Ely, Minnesota
May, 1990

A Creature of Wisdom and Power

In every area of the world where people live with bear — or observe it from afar — it sparks the human imagination and inspires deep emotion. In those breathtaking moments when the bear rises majestically to its hind legs, it seems much more vital, graceful, and transcendent than a person. Bears can also be frightening, irascible, clumsy, or funny, but they always seem, somehow, to know more than we do.

People in many cultures share a belief that bears possess wisdom and power, and among native cultures, few other animals have been honored with as much ritual attention. Hunting customs, ceremonial feasts, the wearing of bear hides and costumes, and the depiction of bears in art, song, story, and dance signify the bear's importance to people throughout the Northern Hemisphere.

Native peoples' day-to-day observations of the bear's great strength and sharp senses, as well as its survival skills, intelligence, and excellent memory might have stimulated beliefs about its power. Northeast Asian peoples referred to the bear as "owner of the earth." At home in water, trees, caves, and underground, the bear had no natural enemies and was master of all domains. Mysteriously appearing wherever food was available, bears seemed to have an uncanny sense of the cycle of budding leaves, emerging grasses, hatching insects, spawning fish, falling nuts, and ripening berries.

People have been trying to explain the mysteries of hibernation for quite some time. Native peoples' observations of hibernating bears may have inspired beliefs in its extraordinary powers of renewal and immortality. Buried in its winter den, the bear appeared to die, only to revive and emerge in triumphant good health in the spring. The Shoshoni people believed that the deep thunder of early spring indicated that sleeping bears were awakening in their dens, signalling the time for spring celebrations of renewal.

The names of many North American wild

Bear-ly Known
Ojibwa, 1989
Jeffrey Chapman

Artist Jeffrey Chapman spoke of the bear's symbolic significance and about his work:

"Makwa Manido, the bear spirit and a guardian of the Great Medicine Lodge of the Midewiwin of the Anishinabe (Ojibwa) people, is always considered the embodiment of strength and power. In the past, men of the Bear Clan were noted for their exploits in war.

My use of the bear is both as symbol and as creature. As a living creature, the bear is rarely seen, and is more likely to be known only as tracks in the sand. Bears were also once thought to die each fall and be reborn each spring. This in itself was proof of their power.

The bear as symbol is the bear that walks upright and lives both inside and outside of men and the world. The bear exists outside of the world of modern 'civilized' cultures, but even today, continues to live inside the hearts of modern people, whose ancestors wore claws as symbols of courage."

plants, such as bear's tongue, bear's wort, bear's tail, bear's paw, bear clover, bear's ear, bear's breech, bear moss, bear corn, bear bane, and bearberry, may reflect the bear's widespread association with medicine and healing. Bears forage very intently, and people who watched them may have concluded that bears exercised a medicinal craft as they culled and sifted the plant and animal foods that would strengthen and sustain them. Bears were believed to concoct mixtures of special plants, stomp them into a mush, and consume them as restoratives, and when hunters found well-healed wounds on the carcass of a freshly skinned bear, they assumed that it had soothed itself with poultices of roots, leaves, saliva, and mud. For stomach complaints, bears ate ants.

Some Native American cultures believed that bears knew—and could be coaxed to divulge—the best places in which to sow tobacco. Many rites show a connection between bears and tobacco, which was often smoked in ceremonial pipes and shared with the bear's spirit.

Bear Rituals in Native Cultures

One of the oldest and most deeply-rooted of all legends explains a deep connection between bears and humankind. Numerous variations of The Story of the Bear Mother (or The Bear Sons) have been told since ancient times in cultures throughout the world. The Haida people of British Columbia relate a typical version, which begins when a young woman spills a basket of berries she is picking. A stranger wearing a bear cloak offers her assistance and leads her to a hidden place deep underground. Once inside, the woman is frightened by the inhabitants—humans in bearskins who transform themselves into bears whenever they leave the cave. The woman is told that she will be killed unless she marries the bear chief's son. She does so and learns to love her bear husband. Before long, she bears and suckles twin sons who are half human and half bear. One day, the bear husband, who has dreamt that his wife's brothers will kill him,

Bear effigy pipe and pipestem
Ojibwa, 1989
Robert Rose-Bear

Pipestone (catlinite) bowl with lead inlay. Sumac stem, with black bear claws and fur, ermine tails, silver cones, deerskin, and glass beads. The Science Museum of Minnesota.

Death of the bear-husband
Haida, 19th century
Courtesy British Columbia Provincial Museum

This sculpture depicts a scene from the bear mother legend told by the Haida people of British Columbia. The legend concerns a woman who marries a bear and gives birth to twin sons that are half human and half bear. Sensing that he will be killed by his wife's brothers, the bear teaches ritual songs to his wife and sons. After the woman's brothers kill the bear, the bear sons become great hunters and teach their mother's people the ritual songs and skills that enable them to hunt successfully. Numerous versions of the bear mother story have been told ancient times in cultures throughout the world.

teaches his wife and the bear sons ritual songs that they must sing when he is killed. Soon afterwards, the woman's brothers, who have been searching desperately for her, kill the bear, who allows himself to be taken without a struggle. When the woman and her sons return to her people, the bear sons shed their bear robes, become great hunters, and teach the tribe to hunt and to perform the special rituals that would renew the bear's spirit and ensure successful hunting.

This ancient story (and its many variations) explains not only kinship between bears and people, but sheds light on the beliefs behind diverse rituals associated with bear hunts in Lapland, Finland, Siberia, Japan, Alaska, British Columbia, and Quebec. Each of these cultures has its own traditions and may hunt black, grizzly, or brown bears, but most bear rituals share common elements of prayer, physical and spiritual preparation for bear hunts conducted according to very strict rules, ceremonial feasts, and reverent disposition of the bear's skull and bones. The bear is deeply valued, not only for its meat and hides, but as the focus for meaningful transactions between people and their deities.

Bear rituals originated in ancient times, but some of them were practiced until quite recently. The Ainu people of Japan performed the ritual *Iyomande* (meaning "to send away"), which involved the sacrifice of a captive bear, until well into this century. The Cree Indians of Quebec continue to honor the black bear during special hunts and feasts. The Canadian Film Board produced a film about these customs in 1973, and a Mistassini Cree illuminated their meaning by telling an interviewer that "If we do not show respect for the bear when we kill him, he will not return."

hese cultures do not view a successful bear hunt as an emblem of human prowess. The people pray, not for the deftness of the hunters, but that the bear will allow itself to be taken. Believing that the bear can hear everything they say, they speak about the hunt in riddles, sometimes describing the kill as "getting hold of" or "reaching" the bear. The bear is given another name, such as "grandfather," "big feet," "black beast," "black food," "the dog of God," "woods dweller," "golden friend," "honey paw," "one who prowls at night," "sticky-mouth," or "unmentionable one." When hunters find the bear—usually in its winter den— they might invite it to come out, and they apologize for killing it. In some cultures, the hunters tell the bear that they are hungry and cold, and need its meat and hide to feed and clothe their families.

After the bear has been killed, the entire community joins in feasting and celebrations of gratitude intended to renew the bear's spirit. The people carefully prepare the bear's meat and parts, cooking, distributing, and eating them according to custom. Because the bear is the most important guest at these celebrations, its skull and hide are usually decorated and placed in a position of honor during the feast. Special music, dances, and reenactments of the hunt are performed at the feasts, which may last for several days.

As an expression of respect for the bear, most cultures carefully dispose of the bear's skull and bones. The Cree Indians, for example, hang the skull, which is most closely connected with the bear's spirit, on a fir tree or a special pole. Other bones are painstakingly wrapped and placed upon a platform where they won't be disturbed, or scavenged by other animals.

Bears, People, and the Great Mystery

"Only to the white man was nature a wilderness and only to him was the land 'infested' with 'wild' animals and 'savage' people. To us it was tame. Earth was bountiful and we were surrounded with the blessings of the Great Mystery."
— Chief Luther Standing Bear
of the Oglala Sioux

When the first European settlers arrived in North America, their view of the new land and its riches and opportunities differed very sharply from those of Native American peoples. The biblical advice—to be fruitful, multiply, and subdue the earth—shaped and justified the conduct of people who considered themselves locked in a treacherous, desperate struggle against the harsh, malevolent forces of nature.

The bear wasn't always regarded as a sublime, intelligent, or benevolent creature, even in Native American tradition. The gullible, foolish bear of Iroquois legend, for example, used his own tail for fishbait and lost it when it froze beneath the surface of a lake. In one Pueblo legend, a bear jeopardized the survival of an entire community by preventing people from gathering berries, seeds, and nuts. Wild Ugly Boy, the hero of the story, won the respect and gratitude of his people by painting himself blue, donning a headdress of hot peppers, and frightening away the bear.

Black bears were the first of many ordeals the settlers encountered. Accounts of those times vividly describe both the real and perceived dangers of bears, as well as the damage they undoubtedly did to crops, foodstores, and livestock. The settlers killed many black bears to protect themselves, and for hides, meat, and sport. As explorers and pioneers pushed westward, the grizzly bear was feared, hated, and exterminated in great numbers.

From the relative safety of a convenient and highly mechanized society, we have begun to question the settlers' ethic—that humans stand apart from other animals and hold inalienable rights to waste and spoil for progress' sake. Deep fear and a sense of competition may have colored our relationship with bears, but the bear will certainly also continue to arouse amazement, respect, affection, and delight. As a potent symbol of the wilderness, the bear may offer us a different understanding of humankind's place in the natural world that we must learn to value, preserve, and protect.

Mimbres bear pottery
Black-on-white bowl
Mimbres, circa 1000-1130
Courtesy the University of Minnesota

Food bowl
Tlingit, circa 1900
Wood, with abalone shell and glass bead inlays
The Science Museum of Minnesota

By applying "Dian Fossey techniques" to learn more about black bear behavior and habitat needs, Dr. Lynn Rogers, shown here with one of his study subjects, and other researchers at the North Central Forest Experiment Station in northern Minnesota have demonstrated the timid and gentle nature of these animals.

K awishiwi. The Ojibway name, we are told, means "no place between." Nothing here, in other words. No population centers, no trading posts, not even a decent hunting ground. No civilized reason to stop along the trail. Typical of the forest cover left over today for the bears.

My kind of country.

I stand here on the bank of the Kawishiwi River in northeastern Minnesota and ponder the connection. Great multitudes of pointed timbers congregate here in silence. Among them the scattered aspens and paper birch and tamarack glow radiant as lamplight in the October evening sun.

The river itself flows northward from here and would, if you let it, carry you deeper toward the heart of the Quetico-Superior Wilderness, a vast expanse of spruce and fir, northern white cedar and red pine, white-tailed deer, moose, timber wolves, beaver, trout, loons, ravens, whisky jacks, retired voyageur routes and disregarded Ojibway spirits. And of course our old friend and current subject, the black bear. Such a trip, taken by a man or woman of proper spirit, would provide not only great joy and challenge, but also a clearer perspective into that which we have forgotten about ourselves, our kindred species, and our own dim past.

In the meantime there is other, more formal research underway here in the Superior National Forest. In fact our sleeping quarters tonight are part of the Kawishiwi Field Lab, North Central Forest Experiment Station, U.S. Forest Service—headquarters for Dr. Lynn Rogers' black bear research.

Rogers has been studying the behavior, travels, demography, habitat requirements, and general design of the black bear of northeastern Minnesota since 1969. He is an expert in the field, you might say. "I'm just trying to learn how they make their living," he says. His study area is hardscrabble country for the bears—long winters, relatively few fruit and nut-bearing hardwoods—and therefore a perfect place in which to carry out his investigations. The truth is always more evident where life is close to the edge.

But why study the black bear in the first place? To provide for its survival, the managers might say. A conceited answer, and only partly true. Left alone, the black bear is entirely capable of finding food, procreating, providing for the survival of its species. It has done so for the past 100,000 years, and under various levels of human hunting pressure for a dozen or so of the most recent millennia. The only threat it cannot handle is the usurpation of its habitat by industrial man and his technologies.

The black bear, like any wild species, functions as a habitat indicator. If its environment is degraded, the population suffers, starves, decreases. Since the black bear lives closer to the land but in similar fashion to man and in much of the same habitat, its population and health provide an index of the quality of the land upon which we, too, depend.

We study the black bear, in part, out of fear. Or rather to dispel it. Here is a legendary (plagued by legends) predator, a carnivore according to phylogenetic order, capable of doing significant damage to tents, automobiles, and picnic lunches, occasionally to livestock, and rarely to humans.

We also study black bears to gain human medical advantage. The physiological endurance of a warm-blooded animal which need not eat or urinate for months of continuous lethargy is a coveted ability. It is also one which, if understood, might suggest treatments for such varying human ailments as gall stones, osteoporosis, diabetes, and severe burns.

We study black bears to learn more about our own behavior. The bears are wild, free, and wildly beautiful as we once were. And still are, sometimes.

And finally, we study them because man has always studied his local bears. It is a habit common to our species, old as the stars.

So much for justification. Human interest in any wild thing is sufficient. Commendable, in fact.

Before bedding down, I make the evening rounds. No bears sighted down by the river or in the compound tonight. Only the steady fall of aspen leaves and that whisper, again, from the pointy timbers. Up there in the farthest north country,

*Throughout the northern latitudes, where bears and humans have coexisted for millennia, bears were the subject of countless myths and legends. One legend that was almost universal among primitive human cultures was that the stars of the constellation **Ursus Major**, the big dipper, outlined the form of a celestial bear.*

however, in what Longfellow called the infinite meadows of heaven, I observe Ursa Major, the Great Bear, making her own silent rounds under cover of darkness and well out of range of Orion (the Hunter!) who stalks the autumn sky south of the zenith—on the wrong side of the hill as always.

A curious penchant, this one for identifying unlikely images in the random heavens. Far more intriguing, however, is the widespread recognition, among human cultures with a view of the northern sky, of a bear (or two, or seven) in the stars surrounding that one we call Polaris. Perhaps, as Shepard and Saunders suggest in *The Sacred Paw*, their treatise on the long-term relationships among bears and men, this and the circumpolar similarities of bear legends and ceremonies practiced by native peoples stem from the great antiquity of mythological origins. By the time man had begun to leave lasting records of his beliefs, this notion of a bear in the boreal stars had percolated from clan to clan, tribe to tribe, culture to culture, around the globe. On evenings just like this one, the legends were recited, embellished, and passed on to anxious, irresponsible teenagers squatting around the fire and looking for trouble. And thus from generation to generation, down through the centuries. The real discoverers of America brought the idea with them across the Bering land bridge 15,000 years ago. Nomadic hunters themselves, they may have been pursuing bears at the time. The cycle was completed when the Europeans stumbled onto the same continent from a different direction and found that the godless savages already inhabiting the place honored the same celestial bear that they did. (A potentially disturbing fact to the Europeans, but one which most were able to ignore.)

How do we explain this exaltation of bears? Why all this infatuation among our progenitors with these cumbersome, myopic brutes which lack, according to current perspective, the cunning of wolves, the genteel grace of deer, the loftiness of eagles?

One thinks first of similarities. Humans have been endowed with many bear-like characteristics, suggesting kinship. Black bears, for example, walk plantigrade—on the soles of their feet—like humans, producing a similar track. They stand on their hind legs on occasion (to see and smell better). They eat many similar foods—sometimes out of the same field, garden, or backpack—and thus occupy a niche similar to that of our species. Black bears suckle their young and provide them care through adolescence. They are accused of being ill-tempered, foul-smelling, independent, asleep for long periods of time, voracious at their feed, and unlikely to stray far from thick cover, ursine characteristics that just about everyone could attribute to a human being of their acquaintance.

The skinned carcass of a black bear hanging from a pole in hunting camp appears remarkably human-like. One can then understand the origin of aboriginal stories of "bear-people" who could take off their skins to appear completely human. Bears were often referred to in human terms among the North American peoples. Cousin, grandfather, or elder, they called him.

From the hide of the black bear came blankets, robes, and covers for the sacred sweat lodges. From its body came food and medicines. Among native peoples the bear became associated with spiritual as well as physical health. Knowledge of black bear denning locations provided many an easy winter foraging trip. The Naskapis tribe of eastern Canada called the bear "black food" and "big great food." The bear itself became big medicine among many peoples, due in part to its winter sleeping habits. To the shaman with no answer to the mysteries of death, here was pretense if not proof of renewal, of life after death, of re-emergence from the sepulcher. To the Chippewas, **Muckwa** the bear was the symbol of rebirth. And to the Bear Clan, the Medicine Bear was the lone guide for men to the River of Meaning. Big medicine.

In short, early man studied the bear for the same reasons we study them today. Little has changed, except that somewhere along the line our course of living has diverged dramatically from that

When nervous black bears are hesitant to approach food near people, they may lunge and explosively expel air while slapping the ground or surrounding vegetation. Lynn Rogers and other researchers have witnessed this startling and sometimes frightening display many times. Never, however, has the display been followed by an attack. A black bear wades in the broad Kawishiwi River near the U.S. Forest Service's Kawishiwi Field Laboratory near Ely.

of the bears. We, and, I speak in general terms here, no longer sniff the wind for food or enemy, sleep under the stars, or forage in the forest for tubers and grubs. Using our own modern mythology and a variety of artifice, we have succeeded in separating ourselves from the real world, divorcing our distant beginnings. It wasn't easy.

Meanwhile, back at the Kawishiwi, evening rounds are over and still no earthly bears to be found. As a final test of the ancient hypothesis I put my questions to that ethereal ursine up there in her meadow.

"Good evening, old bear," I say to her.

I detect a distant twinkle.

"Show me that River of Meaning, will you? Can we ever follow it home again? What can you tell us, eh?"

As usual, she declines to answer. Oblivious to all, she continues only to point out the pole star and certify our latitude with her position above the steepled forest, giving us a few bearings and nothing more. No matter. I have other sources.

Earlier today, for example, I consulted with Dr. Rogers himself and a two-and-a-half-year-old female black bear named Patch who inhabits a territory not far from here.

Six of us has tramped into the bush, following Rogers' chief field technician, Greg Wilker, and his classic antenna. Choosing his direction from the signal in his headphones and the lay of the land, Greg backtracked and circled about. He called the bear by name. Were he alone, Rogers said, he might have walked straight to her.

This is the new research technique, Rogers explained. After years of radio-tracking bears by truck and airplane, Rogers came up with a new and better way to study the bears, one that few others had considered. He would go off into the woods and *watch* them.

Up ahead, Greg had his bear in sight. "Come on, Patch, sit down." The entourage grew nervous with anticipation.

"There you are," said Greg. We climbed up behind him and found his antenna and receiver cached in a young spruce. He was down below with the bear. As we approached, Patch retreated. We took seats. Patch remained hesitant, despite Greg's encouragement. Only twenty-five yards away and in an open understory, the bear was not easy to see.

Embarrassing us all, someone asked that famous but unglamorous question about a bear in the woods. Rogers answered affirmatively. "Every four and half hours, lately," the man of knowledge replied.

Somewhere below us a twig broke. Patch was moving, though it was Greg's footstep we heard. With Greg behind her, she was walking toward us, perhaps recognizing Rogers. One hundred and seventy pounds of bear, coming our way. Not huge, but solid, and rounded by a four-inch radius of fat. Slow but lithe. Her black coat shone with a blue sheen. I detected no odor. She came to within twenty feet of where Lynn and I sat, then hesitated. Rogers spoke to her and tossed a few pieces of bark, hoping she'd think they were "treats" and move closer. Patch recognized the fakery, but approached anyway. At ten feet she stopped, raised her head, tested the air. Not convinced, she moved closer. Rogers tossed more bark, spoke softly to her. She moved beside him.

I felt strangely calm, not because of Rogers' lecture on restraint, but because of the deliberate and tolerant behavior of the bear. I had just begun to contemplate this lack of fear when Patch, who had been looking calmly off to the side, suddenly whirled and slapped a large and well-appointed paw at Rogers, hitting our log immediately next to him and jarring us both. I felt hair standing erect at the base of my neck where I had no hair.

But the bear moved slowly off, calm again, peaceful as a puppy, pausing here and there to sniff after a slug or corm under the leaves, striking an occasional pose for the photographers. Then it disappeared in the undergrowth. Silence among us. I pushed my hackles down.

Native Americans were intrigued by the black bear's ability to hibernate through the "starving moons" of winter. Today medical researchers are studying this aspect of bear physiology in the hope of improving human medicine. Dr. Ralph Nelson (center) of the University of Illinois leads these medical studies. Here he takes a blood sample with Steve Durst (left) and Lynn Rogers. While a research team collects a blood sample and other data from a tranquilized sow, Rogers' wife, Donna, holds three healthy cubs removed from the black bear's den.

"She was just uncomfortable," Rogers said. Nothing more than a signal, a gesture, like a frown. No contact made or intended. "Most people would play that up, but it's really the mildest expression of uneasiness," he said. "Black bears use a lot more restraint than even I gave them credit for."

Has Patch ever made contact? I asked. Yes, a few times, but only with a scolding slap like she might use to belt a cub or a sibling. Never anything near an attack. Have any of the study bears ever attacked? "Never," said Lynn. "That's what I'm trying to tell you."

Next morning Greg and I leave the crowd behind. In his study vehicle, the standard field biologist's truck—sun-faded green four-by-four, driver's seat cover worn from the constant mount and dismount, a bit loose around the crankcase—we rumble down another dirt track through a mosaic of boreal forest and squared meadows of regenerating birch thickets (commercial cuttings). Twice we stop for Greg to point to the four winds with his antenna. He wants to see how close we can get to Terry, a female littermate of Patch who has recently begun conditioning. No luck. A light rain is falling and Terry is on the move. Searching out her last bites of clover or fleabane, perhaps, and already beginning to conserve the energy she's assimilated into fat throughout the summer and early autumn. Possibly looking for a den site. We backtrack, take another road.

Greg pulls off the track and into the trees, kills the engine. Terry's signal is loud in the phones this time. We move in on her. Greg carries his receiver and antenna, and I am left holding a bucket of cubed beef fat. Encouragement for the trainee.

Under a light drizzle we move across a dome of Ely greenstone— ancient and rugged country, and therefore more precious and attractive. Greg observes a fresh bear dropping. Based on his own observations, he believes black bears regularly defecate at certain points as a means of scent marking, though he recognizes that their anal glands are not as thoroughly developed as those of, say, the timber wolf. Not yet, anyway, I suggest. We must remember that, like humans and other more recent and yet imperfect species, the black bear is still in the throes of evolution, still specializing. "They're already pretty special to me," says Greg.

A few yards away we find a vague dish of leaves and sticks between the roots of a huge white pine. A bear's nest, likely constructed by a sow last spring. The cubs would rest here and use the tree for safety.

Now we move down through the alder whips and into a bowl-shaped depression in the otherwise hilly terrain. Greg thought of the bog when we didn't find Terry where he'd left her last. By October the bears travel less, slow down to conserve energy, and seek dens. With the virtual disappearance of fruits and nuts here by late September, Greg surmised that the bear might move to the swamp for a meal of the last available green vegetation.

We make our way through the familiar complex of sphagnum moss, snowberry, Labrador tea, and black spruce that lines this four-acre basin. At one end of the bog is a stand of mature black ash.

"There she is," says Greg. "Come here, Terry. It's okay. . . " We move into a thicket of spruce after the retreating bear. Bowing to look closely at a depression in the foliage, I see the moss lofting in the fresh absence of bear carcass. "TERRY, cut it out," Greg says.

Through the spruces, scramble up a rock outcrop, and back down into the bog. Another merry chase, I see. "This is the first stage in turning a wild bear into a bear like Patch," says Greg, pulling dead branches from his Yagi antenna. He points it about, moves off again. In a dense thicket ahead we hear movement. Greg moves in saying, "Come on, Terry . . . . Come on, Terry . . . ," sounding more like a big brother than a scientist. He catches another glimpse of her, but then she is gone. We circle again through the bog, pursuing a barefoot animal of my weight that is eluding us in silence. The rain intensifies.

People and black bears share similar characteristics in size and skeletal structure and, as well as eating many of the same foods, leave similar, five-toed tracks. Bears also sometimes assume human-like postures when sitting or standing on their hind feet. Because of these similarities to our own species, Native Americans sometimes referred to black bears as "brother" or "grandmother" or similar appelations.

She'll stop soon, according to Greg. He's seen her legs shaking. In preparation for hibernation, her circulatory system has already begun to reduce the blood supply to her extremities. "They let you find them on their terms," he says, "where they want you to." Then he resumes his patient tracking and his "Come on, Terry" commentary.

After two and a half laps our guided tour ends on a faint game trail in the dankest gut of the bog. In a small clearing ahead of us I see the sheen of another blue-black coat. There is a bear inside. She has stopped, and Greg seems to hold her there by voice and visual contact. We kneel in the muck. He tosses her a lump of fat, keeps talking to her. Terry moves our way, investigating, shins a few feet up a large spruce, checks her horizons, climbs back down, comes closer. Comes very close, in fact, right up to us, all the while appearing to exercise great caution. Operating, one might say, with careful consideration. Much like myself. I hand Greg another piece of fat which he offers to her and which, after a long pause, she takes from his hand. Ever so gently.

I admire the fullness and cleanness of her coat, the grace and strength with which she moves her bulk beneath it. I feel a desire to run my fingers through that fur, to grasp a roll of hide like I would the skin of an old bird dog—with affection. A foolish but human desire. I forgive myself immediately and remember, in turn, my fear.

As Greg reaches to offer another morsel he shifts his weight and a twig crackles underfoot. Terry wheels about and rushes off fifteen or twenty feet, stops, turns. Suddenly calm, she gazes off to the side, away from us. For a moment. Electricity builds. *Deja vu.* I know what's coming now. Much as expected, the bear blows, lunges forward, slams both front feet to the ground. Despite yesterday's lesson and all my careful notes, my first thought is that this bear could mean business, this could be the exception, the refutation of Rogers' hypothesis. I think of statistics—my own vital statistics. The hackles rise again. Someone is pounding a drum in my ears. Meanwhile, Terry sees

the bucket.

She moves close—no sense waiting for an invitation now—between Greg and me. Pushes between us. And I'm thinking, "What the hell, there might be something to this restraint theory—there'd better be." And besides, there's no way out. And besides, we're here to learn something; let's not tamper with the experiment. Greg, meanwhile, appears pleasantly surprised. Careful and still, but calm.

"She's getting into the fat," I whisper. (He can't see her now; she's behind him, the dense fur of her neck pressed against my thigh.) "Don't let her," he says.

Right.

Terry finishes the fat while I carefully hold the bucket's handle so that it doesn't fall and lock the thing to her head. She backs away. Should have rationed the fat, Greg says quietly, then reminds me that she may return and slap him on the arm out of mild disappointment that there is no more to eat. I remind him that I am the one holding the bucket. But I also note that everything so far has gone smoothly, theory or no. If Terry does take a swat at one of us, I will understand.

But she does not. Instead she blows loudly and roughs up a small spruce nearby. Hackles again. And Greg says to her, "Oh, such a mean bear." No sweat.

She backs off and Greg talks to her for several more minutes, then approaches her one more time, watching carefully for the little signs that would tell him he is too close. He wants this visit to end on good terms—optimum conditioning for a subject of study. He offers his cap, inquires about her den. She licks his hand, looking for suet.

I feel a rush of warmth now. Relief, in part. And a certain pride. I have touched the empirical bear. Or rather it has touched me, and the reality of the world, fierce and beautiful, seems, at least for the moment, closer.

Our little rendezvous ends as it began, on the bear's terms. Terry parts company by casually

A receiver and directional antenna show the way to a radio collared bear's den. Each bear has its own identifying radio frequency. Researchers change the bear's radio-collar every two years before batteries expire. Some collared bears have been radio-tracked continuously for more than twenty years. Photo by Ed Linquist. Black bears weigh less than they appear to in fall, when thick underfur makes their long guard hairs stand almost straight out. Four people guessed this female at three hundred and fifty to five hundred pounds. Actual weight: one hundred and twelve pounds.

foraging in a different direction, looking back at us periodically through those little brown watery—but attentive—eyes. I find at best a rough correlation here, in an evolutionary sense and difficult to articulate, between the bear and me. My natural reaction—call it biological respect—is precisely the kind of behavior which reinforced the bears' restraint across thousands of years of evolution.

There is one other sensation. Looking into the bear's eye I found paradox: the familiarity of a brown mammalian eye, yet a portal to an entirely different world of being. A world I can never know, a perspective which, no matter how I position myself, I shall never quite grasp. I feel for a moment like Orion—always a little too late and on the wrong inclination to catch his quarry. But there is no failure here, rather a re-awakening of wonder, that vital complement to cold academic pursuit. Perhaps this is what we've forgotten from our past more than anything—to allow for what Barry Lopez called "a tolerance for mysteries." And perhaps this is, unknowingly, the most compelling reason for studying the black bear.

At thirty yards her shape diminishes silently through the rain and into the alder bush, and like the stars at first morning light, she disappears.

Terry, one of Lynn Rogers' study bears, appears threatening in her stare and steady approach. As she approaches him and his camera, however, she is only investigating to see if he has brought her a treat.

CHAPTER 2

OF TIME AND THE COLD WOODS

The black bear's behavior, anatomy and physiology have evolved as a result of its existence in cold, northern climates. Because its food consists mainly of plant material, the black bear's annual cycle of activities is dictated by the annual cycle of plant growth in those same habitats.

A Natural History

The black bear, *Ursus americanus*, the "bear of America," is named for the continent on which it is found. Of the three species of bears currently inhabiting North America, only the black bear is found exclusively here and nowhere else. And only the black bear evolved to its current specific form on the face of this continent—a true native. Both the grizzly (brown) bear and the polar bear became what they are in Asia and emigrated across the Bering Land Bridge hundreds of millennia after the black bear's ancestors had crossed.

The black bear (order Carnivora) is not a practicing carnivore as its official taxonomy would indicate. It is a legitimate omnivore with borderline herbivorous tendencies. The truth about its diet has been known for decades, but frequently misrepresented. Even the earlier literature, noted A.W. Schorger in 1949, sometimes described the black bear as a strict vegetarian to discredit alleged livestock depredation. It may still be most famous in certain circles for bringing down and devouring large prey including—extremely rarely—humans, but the black bear is far more commonly observed stalking a meal of unsuspecting clover and bedstraw, blackberries, beechnuts, or apples and sweetcorn if the others fail. The black bear occasionally preys on deer, elk, moose calves, sheep, cattle, and defenseless backpacks—but generally only when its regular foods are hard to come by and the quarry is hindered by deep snow, disease, or a stock fence. Much of the red meat the black bear consumes is already dead and often infested with the little writhing pearl-colored carnivores which found it first. Unsavory? Quite the opposite to the black bear, whose chief source of animal protein comes from its primary prey: insects.

The carnivore title persists because the phylogenetic roots of *Ursus americanus* can be traced backwards through the depths of fossil history to a juncture at which the family of bears (Ursidae) split from the carnivorous stock from which it is derived.

The carnivorous reputation persists because enough of the black bear's predatory characters have: strength, claws, canines, and speed in bursts up to thirty miles per hour. The black bear retains a share of the ability, and occasionally the desire, to exercise the carnivorous option.

But not that much of the ability, we are told. "The black bear can digest meat, but is poor at catching it," writes Lynn Rogers. Too much bulk, legs too short, wrong attitude. "Most of what it catches are newborn animals that it happens onto while feeding on vegetation or insects." No longer a hunter, a carnivore by name only.

How the modern black bear came to this contradiction between taxonomic order and ecological adaptations is an interesting story, but rather lengthy—about four epochs long.

Approximately twenty-five million years ago, in what is known as the Miocene epoch of the Tertiary period of earth history (a time when sabre-toothed cats were peacefully stalking the early grazing mammals under tropical skies), a distinct line of mammals which would give rise to our bears diverged from the Miacidae, a family of small tree-climbing predators from which would later evolve the wolf family.

(Twenty-five million years may sound like a long time, impossible to comprehend for most. But not so, the paleogeologists tell us. They work with a time scale which reaches in reverse direction some five billion years to the point at which the earth's crust hardened. The Miocene, they say, was a rather recent development.)

This divergent stock was first represented in fossil evidence by an animal the size of a fox terrier in subtropical Europe, twenty million years ago: *Ursavus elemensis*. *Ursavus* remained in the forest but became more omnivorous, gradually evolving to eat primarily highly digestible vegetable matter. This change in diet was facilitated by a lengthening of the intestine from the relatively short gut of the true carnivores. Animal food is about twice as easily digested as plant matter; lengthening the digestive

---

When threatened, black bears are more likely to retreat up trees than to attack. This "escape attitude" probably became inbred during the millennia that black bear faced the short-faced bear (now extinct), a predacious and more-powerful bear that could not climb trees. As winters lengthened and became more severe with the coming of the Ice Ages, plant and insect foods were only seasonally available. Consequently, black bears evolved an ability to store fat and to hibernate during these periods of food shortage. Only occasionally predatory, black bears eat mainly fruit, nuts, vegetation, and insect larvae. Their long canine teeth are used most often to tear apart logs and other objects to obtain insect larvae.

tube gives the body more time to dissolve and incorporate that which is eaten. Today the black bear and the grizzly retain a longer digestive system in ratio to body length (8:1) than does the wolf (4:1), but one still short and unspecialized when compared to the ruminant system. The bear's teeth also show a mild swing toward a primarily vegetarian diet. The shearing, carnassial premolars and molars are gone, replaced by crushing bunodont molars and the diminutive vestigial premolars. The teeth are not so specialized for vegetables, however, as those of the moose.

Back to antiquity. About six million years ago, approximately halfway through the Pliocene epoch, as earth's warm climate gradually cooled, a huge bear-like form, *Indarctos*, likely the first in its line to immigrate to North America, roamed the Old World forests. Along with it lived a smaller line, *Protursus*, more adept at climbing and from which the bears of the genus *Ursus* would descend. The first of these in fossil record appeared in Europe later in the Pliocene as the Auvergne bear, *Ursus minimus*. During Auvergne's reign, two events are noted. Interesting but inconsequential at the time was the first appearance of *Homo erectus* at least one and one-half million years before present. Far more important, just as Auvergne was grading into the Etruscan bear (*Ursus etruscus*) one million years or so ago, earth's slowly chilling climate reached a threshold. Peering over the horizon was the Pleistocene—the ages of ice.

Etruscan stock give rise to the black, brown, and cave bears. Earliest identified among these was Deninger's cave bear, which dates to some seven hundred thousand years ago and which may have crossed trails with *Homo erectus*. Deninger's gave rise to the true cave bear (*Ursus spelaeus*), a huge browsing animal of Europe and Russia, referred to as "the most bearish of bears" by Bjorn Kurten, who made the species famous. In the late Pleistocene, the cave bear and Neanderthal man (an early race of *Homo sapiens*) evidently met, interacted, and established an informal association of mutual respect.

This relationship lasted forty thousand years or more and likely engendered the bear cults which became characteristic features of ancient northern cultures. The cults themselves survived; the cave bear and the Neanderthal did not.

Meanwhile, during the early Pleistocene, some of the Etruscan stock had immigrated at their earliest opportunity into North America and engendered several varieties. One of these, the Florida cave bear (*Tremarctos floridanus*, strikingly similar to the cave bears of Europe but separately descended), survived to share time with early man here. It vanished southward to reappear, somewhat remodeled, as the Andean or spectacled bear of the same genus in South America today.

The huge short-faced bear (*Artodus simus*) also appeared on the continent in the early Pleistocene, approximately one million years ago. A brutal, long-legged, and highly predacious animal of uncertified origins, this bear would have outweighed and outrun the modern Kodiak. It apparently dominated the continent and particularly interfered with the livelihoods of those bears which had left the safety of the forest.

The earliest evidence of the genus *Ursus* in North America was found in a cave near Port Kennedy, Pennsylvania. Here lay the last skeletal remains—at least five hundred thousand years old—of what may be an intergrade between the Etruscan and today's black bear. By contrast, our brown bears, of Asian-Etruscan decent, appeared in the New World within the last one hundred thousand years and confined themselves to the Alaska area until the short-faced bear disappeared. Polar bears splintered off from the brown bear line in Asia and also arrived later.

During the Pleistocene, several periods of glaciation occurred across North America and Eurasia. The glaciers tied up much water in ice, dropping sea levels and thereby opening the land bridge between Siberia and Alaska. This land area, known as Beringia when above water, facilitated at least three crossings of bear stock (*Indarctos*, Etruscan,

Unlike black bears, polar bears are most active in winter when they can ambush seals at breathing holes. Polar bears fatten in winter, rather than summer. Ironically, polar bears have black skin and black bears have light skin. On following page: Bears give birth to smaller young, compared to the mother's size, than any other placental mammal. Hibernation physiology retards fetal growth, so mothers give birth after only two months of fetal development and nurse their non-hibernating cubs in what some people aptly term an "external pregnancy."

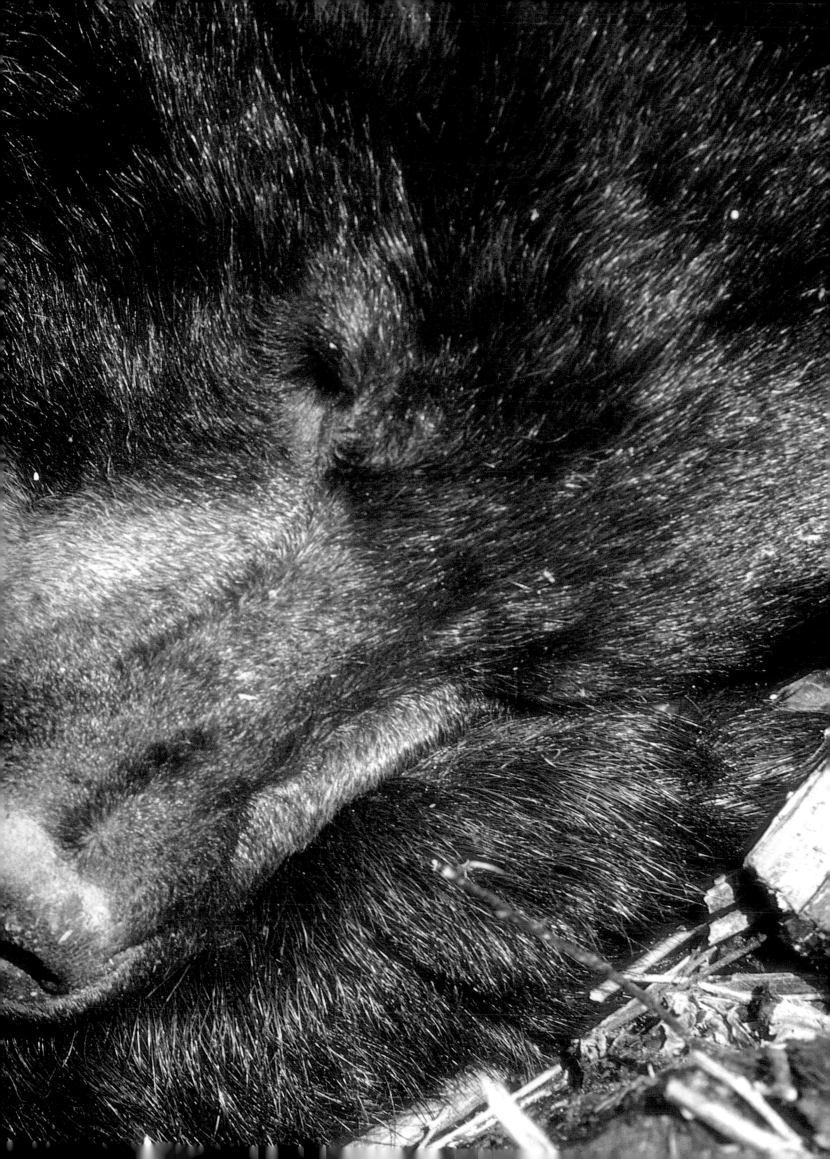

brown) and at least one, probably more, of wandering bands of *Homo sapiens*. Not only did the Pleistocene provide a bridge allowing immigration of Old World mammals into North America, it also provided the second major factor which shaped the evolution of the black bear. (The first was the forest biome itself, in which the original bear stock arose and in which the early black bears found food and escape from the short-faced bear.) I refer now to the advent of a cold season in the climate.

Pleistocene bears that maintained or developed heat-conserving mechanisms tended to survive this environmental condition. One such mechanism is increased body size: A larger animal has a lower ratio of surface area to volume, and thus a relatively lower rate of heat loss. According to Bergmann's Rule, a standard biological theory, one would expect to find larger individuals of the same species in cooler areas. Indeed, Kurten found evidence that throughout the ice ages, cave bear body sizes varied inversely with the cycling climatic temperatures. Other mechanisms bears utilize for heat conservation include a thick fur coat, deposition of subcutaneous fat, and the shortening of extremities to reduce surface area. Each of these, however, appeared by way of trade-off with carnivorous skills. The accompanying loss of agility, reach, and speed further reduced the predatory nature of the animal.

Our ancestral black bears, then, found sufficient nutritional gain by relying predominantly on highly digestible vegetative foods. With the advent of an earth year containing a cold period during which such vegetable matter (lush grasses, fruit, nuts, starch-laden tubers) was either unavailable or out of production, we arrive in our discussion at the most complex and unique—some would say miraculous—portion of this bear's natural history.

Consider the problem: In order to maintain a constant body temperature, the warm-blooded bear required a constant source of food for energy. Pleistocene winters interrupted this food source while providing conditions for greater heat loss. Even in areas in which snow did not fall, many of the plants would adapt to a cooler season by producing new growth and flowering bodies primarily during the warmer seasons—a cycle reinforced by periodic cooling of the climate, which selected for those plants suited to seasonal growth and production. The answer, of course, for a number of animals which relied on foods available only during warm periods and which were not prepared to migrate, was a period of dormancy during the food shortage.

But the bears were confounded in yet another way. Like other large mammals, they had adopted a strategy for survival which required a great amount of care for a relatively small and slowly maturing litter. The low reproductive rate was balanced with the slow and careful development of the cubs, a development which required more than a year.

In order to store enough fat to survive their first winter of hibernation, cubs would then have to be ready to begin feeding and growing in the spring. A unique problem: No other family of mammals adapting to winter food shortages with some form of dormancy must also have its young emerge immediately in the spring. Bears became the only creatures to endure pregnancy during hibernation.

Most hibernating animals undergo a reduction of body temperature to near freezing during winter sleep, but arise every few days or so to stretch limbs, peel open their eyes, nibble on the food cache, and stumble off to relieve bladder and bowels. A pregnant animal could not follow this system. At near zero Celsius, with all maternal systems at emergency low idle, how could the fetuses develop?

Current summary of discussion: Under a seasonal existence, the bear's life equation came to require hibernation and the emergence of cubs immediately after dormancy in the spring. This required winter gestation, which in turn required a warm dormancy unlike the frigid sleep of other hibernators. And it required "premature" birth of young so that the mother could efficiently transfer energy to the cubs through milk rather than through

This two-week-old cub has doubled its birthweight but still weighs less than two pounds. Its eyes will remain closed for another two to five weeks until it can walk. Its ears are still laid back, as they were at birth. The mouth opening is still small, an adaptation for sucking, but the claws are developing rapidly to aid climbing when the cub leaves the den at about three months of age. Like most babies, newborn cubs have blue eyes. Black bear cubs cry out when they are cold or they find themselves alone. The mother bear, usually nearby, will come quickly to the plaintive cries of her offspring. When their teeth begin to come in, black bear cubs, much like puppies and teething children, chew whatever is available.

placental transfer, which is more costly to the mother, given the limitations of hibernating physiology. Black and brown bears today give birth in January or February after a short gestation period, then suckle the tiny cubs through the winter.

So much for parturition, now to the important issue. When to breed? The Pleistocene dictated again. If bears need to feed solidly and continuously during that time of year when the most highly nutritional and easily digestible vegetable foods are available—late summer through autumn—in order to store enough energy to survive winter anorexia, then the only time remaining for the complexities of mammalian sex is late spring or early summer. And, indeed, our bears today breed in June and early July, rarely elsewise.

One final fine-tuning of this unique life equation remains. Breeding occurs in early summer, but the actual implantation of the blastocyst (an early stage of the embryo) onto the uterine wall does not occur until November. While it may keep gestation requirements out of the intense autumn feeding period and help delay births until winter, this technique of delayed implantation also allows for an escape from pregnancy. In terms of biological theory, the act of breeding presupposes maternal physiological capability. ("If you can conceive it, you can raise it.") But bears depend on food sources that can vary highly from year to year. Drought or late frost can restrict the availability of precisely that provender which bears require. While the real carnivores and browsers are largely subject to longer-term forage trends, bears must react to differing annual potentials, the most critical of which may be expressed months after the breeding trysts. If by late autumn the female fails to lay on enough fat for her own survival and the gestation and nursing of her young, her reproductive physiology is likely to prevent the blastocysts from implanting and developing into what might become a fatal energy drain for her. Rather than risk the loss of her productive life, she will simply wait until next year.

What of all this physiological theory? To what end this discussion of pale and distant antiquity? Simply this: Together they point out how the current specifications of *Ursus americanus* were engineered through its longtime attachment to the forest biome and "recent" adaptations to a cold season. And what of the paradox of the black bear's carnivore title? Why, it's not really a paradox after all, but a rather blatent shortcoming of phylogenetic nomenclature. And the bear's miraculous life history? Nothing more than simple, natural evolutionary design. Explainable, if surprising, and as commonplace as most other miracles of life. Therein lies their beauty.

The Pleistocene glaciers had one more pronounced effect on the genus *Ursus* in North America. Because the glaciers invaded and retreated across the land masses of the northern hemisphere not once but several times, they incidentally provided a new habitat. Open tundra and treeless plains remained behind each withdrawing ice mass. It is widely accepted that some of the bears took advantage of the succulent growth (and grazing animals) on the open lands, and that this line became the brown bears, including our much beloved grizzly. The primary physical and behavioral differences which we currently observe between the grizzly and black bears are explainable using this hypothesis.

While the black bear retained the curved claw for climbing in the forest and rolling over logs, the grizzly's forebears developed straighter, longer claws better suited for digging tubers, corms, and ground squirrels and their caches, out on the plains. As the claws straightened and these bears left the forest, they forfeited their escape route into the overstory, supplanting it with a more aggressive demeanor for the protection of cubs. An aggression backed up by the huge claws, extremely strong forelegs, larger size, and those old formidable canines. Both the black and the grizzly retained their speed for defense: the grizzly to face a perceived threat, and the black bear to escape it.

Black bears usually mate in June, about the same time they molt their winter coats, but fertilized eggs do not implant and begin fetal development until November. If a female is too lean in fall, her eggs will not implant, saving her the physiological expense of developing young during hibernation. Black bear digging is typically limited to turning over sod to find junebeetle larvae. Digging for roots and rodents is a behavior more typical of grizzly bears, which also commonly also dig their winter dens. Less than half of all black bears dig dens for hibernation. Because black bear cubs can readily climb trees, which are usually available in much of their habitat, they do not require, as do grizzly cubs in their typically treeless habitat, an aggressive defense from their mother for protection from predators. Grizzly sows, on the other hand, very aggressively defend their young.

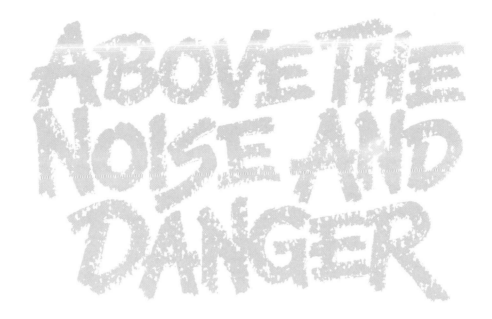

CHAPTER 3

ABOVE THE
NOISE AND
DANGER

These two bears are actually threatening each other, not fighting. Bears often use the same communicative displays toward people that they use to communicate with each other.

"Most fear of bears comes from reading too much scare literature, talking to too many people who are afraid of them (it's catching) and spending too little time with actual bears."

— Dr. Lynn Rogers

"The Bearman knoweth."

— Anonymous

At the heart of our intrigue with the black bear lies our romance with the species. And at the very heart of this romance, if truly a romance, we find a dark and primal fear. In this case, the fear of attack. Like the wolf and the lion, the bear provides allegory for the ferocity in our literature, biblical and otherwise. "I will fall upon them like a bear robbed of her cubs, I will tear open their breast . . . ," wrote Hosea in the Old Testament, quoting Someone Else at the time. That was years ago in a distant land. Yet the image of a large, hair-covered, nearly humanoid creature rearing from the shadows with fierce countenance and bared carnassials persists in our human psyche. This in spite of the far more common sight of an ursine hind-end rolling into the nearest cover, bent on escape. (The black bear's brain contains images too.)

"Bears may be the most feared of North American animals," Dr. Barrie Gilbert wrote recently in a technical paper on black bear aggression. He based his assertion on simple common knowledge. Because of the well-known aggressiveness of the grizzly, he noted, many people tend to dread any bear. Given our modern penchants for generalizing facts and hyperbolizing rumor, who can be surprised?

We may, however, qualify our bear phobias, at least on the northwestern quadrant of our continent where grizzly and black bear ranges overlap. "Most people don't fear black bears as they do grizzlies," writes Stephen Herrero. In his Canadian view, "This bear rightfully never became the topic of fearsome legend."

And in fact, today we find thousands of urban and suburban inhabitants who venture forth into the roadsides, campgrounds, and backcountry of state, federal, and provincial parks each year, starved for a closeness to the wild. What began on this continent in the 1940s as an improvement in ecological understanding, when Aldo Leopold shed new light on the "evil predator" mentality, has strayed in certain circles to an equally erroneous caricature of predators as purported by the video screen images of Gentle Ben, Grizzly Adams, and Smokey the Bear. And innocent campers still appear shocked, sometimes frightened, to learn that the real bears don't always conform to media caricatures.

This is not an unusual American paradox. If we don't know what to believe, we embrace both extremes, calling on each as the occasion affords. The same bear that endears himself to tourists by begging for food along the roadways of the Great Smokey Mountains National Park will be shot as a fearsome marauder by a posse of townsfolk a mile outside the park boundary.

Further clouding the issue, bear attack stories of nightmarish intrigue jump out at us from the popular press. Even our national parks in Canada and the U.S., attempting to dissolve liability and avoid litigation, now tender serious warnings of possible bear-inflicted injury to every man, woman, and child passing through their gates.

Everyone likes a good bear story, and some of us, as the park services recognize from experience, need one. Or several. For the best collection of verified accounts of bear attacks, including analyses of behaviors and gruesome details (necessary for the analyses), read Stephen Herrero's *Bear Attacks*. Herrero, a professor of biology at the University of Calgary, offers us the most readable and objective treatment of the subject. One warning, however: The details and descriptions will, as always, tend to overshadow the realistic unlikelihood of bona fide attacks.

Herrero would be the first of many in the field to tell you that black bear attacks are extremely rare. In the rural and semi-urban areas of

Bears stuffed in ferocious-looking postures, exhibiting unnatural dog-like snarling and attack behaviour, and excessive warnings in government brochures make it difficult for people to think realistically about black bear behavior. Much of our intrigue with black bears comes from their power and our fear of them. This large male looks menacing as he curls his snout and bares the large canine teeth he inherited from his ancestors twenty-five million years ago. As fearsome as its expression is, though, this bear is only wrinkling its nose to get rid of a bothersome stable fly.

Pennsylvania, for example, an area shared by high population levels of bears and humans, Gary Alt is unable to find a single documented case of human injury by a wild black bear since 1900. In New Hampshire, bear biologist Eric Orff found only two documented human fatalities caused by black bears—both more than two hundred years ago. The last "attack" in New Hampshire occurred fifteen years ago. Feeling crowded even then, a Lakes Region bear of moderate means exercised the ambition of many a local native and ran a surveyor up a tree. Or so the story goes.

Many alleged attacks by black bears are misinterpretations of what the bear had in mind. In other words, most people who climb trees to escape black bears do so unnecessarily. If the bear wanted them, it would climb the tree. So why the reports? "People do not fear what the black bears do, but what they think they might do," Gary Alt told me. Lynn Rogers agrees. "People mainly interpret everything a bear does out of their own fear," says Rogers.

In the backcountry, black bears depend upon their superior nose and hearing to sense the approach of humans, in order to avoid them. Naturally wary of humans, black bears appear to be generally more timid in the eastern U.S. than elsewhere. Here, it can be surmised, the more aggressive bears were removed from the gene pool for generations, a selection process amplified by the population reduction imposed by habitat loss as the forests were cleared. The populations here today would then be the posterity of the few timid bears which survived by hiding in the vestiges of woodland. Western and northern black bears' behavioral heredity is probably not so affected by European man, but may have endured a similar selective pressure while evolving in the shadow of the grizzly for thousands of years.

Even bears at dumps rarely attack their human audience. "It's hard to tease a bear with so much food around," says Lynn Rogers, who has studied the situation. "While it's mostly the largest,

dominant males which come to dumps to feed, people are generally very safe watching them." Black bears rarely want people, Gary Alt told me in simple terms, therefore they rarely catch any.

The fact is, bears—especially black bears—interact with humans at a high frequency across North America, particularly where bears feed on human foods, such as at garbage dumps and public parks.

Why so? Bears may lose their wariness of humans in either of two ways or, as often is the case, a combination of both. Through habituation to the presence of nonaggressive humans in bear country, bears lose their natural fear of people. Food conditioning, on the other hand, is the process by which bears learn to seek human foods when rewarded with human foods for their efforts.

Even where humans and black bears meet each other up close and frequently, such as in Yosemite and Great Smokies National Parks, the bears show extreme tolerance toward human behavior. For example, less than six percent of black bear-human interactions in 1978 and 1979 in Yosemite involved bear aggression, according to researcher Barrie Gilbert. And the majority of aggressive behavior involved a only small number of bears. "Most of the black bears in our study showed little aggression toward people," he wrote. Mike Pelton, in contrast, observed up to forty percent aggressive behaviors of bears toward roadside tourists in Great Smokey Mountain National Park, where people often crowd the bears in an effort to get closer to them. Given the latitude in definition of such terms as "aggression" and "encounter," this difference is not surprising. Most attacks occur where people feed bears, tease them, and try to pet them, says Lynn Rogers.

Parallel to findings of most other black bear aggression studies, Gilbert found that most reported bear "attacks" were bluffs or false charges intended to carry a message but make no physical contact, although in nearly every case they could have. A study in the Great Smokies concluded that less than

Although this situation looks dangerous, people and black bears have mingled at dozens of garbage dumps like this one for decades without serious injury from bears. Most injuries from black bears that do occur at dumps and at camp sites occur when people crowd around or try to pet hungry bears they are feeding or photographing. Black bears nip or cuff bad-mannered people like they do bad-mannered bears, but injuries from these actions are usually not serious.

six percent of the aggressive encounters themselves ended in any contact by the bears.

This *restraint*, as biologists call it, is the dampening of aggressive behavior, the avoidance of physical contact that could incur injury. Part of the dominant-subordinate behavior common throughout the order Carnivora and other species capable of inflicting mortal injury, restraint probably evolved among members of the same species as a guard against unnecessary mortality, and perhaps to some lesser degree simply to save energy where energy balances are so critical. By relinquishing a battle prior to the possibility of mortal injury, evolutionary scientist Richard E. Leaky asserts, not only is the loser protected from death, but more importantly the winner—the probable contributor to the gene pool—avoids the chance of heavy injury. A perfection in competition has evolved here in which the winner is more likely to survive, and the loser (possibly a subadult testing his prowess) may survive to someday become a winner. In much the same fashion, it is reasonable to conclude that those carnivores which exercised restraint toward members of other powerful species—including humans—survived longer and enhanced the behavioral trait among and within their own species. Restraint, however, is not an absolute certainty; fights to the death and fatal maulings infrequently occur.

Considering the widespread misconceptions of bear attacks in America, I decided I'd better bring the subject up with Rogers. He was in his office at the field lab, scowling into a word processor when I disturbed him. I sensed relief on his part.

Everyone has a bear story, Rogers says. And most "attack" stories include high excitement in the form of the "close call." Restraint, on the part of the bear, he says, provides the perfect setting for chronicles of human bravado. Seeing a bear is memorable enough for most people. And the black bear's bluff charge—another rare event, according to Rogers, and highly subject to misinterpretation—is orchestrated and dramatic. Ears flattened back against its head, upper lip flared and snout narrowed, the bear suddenly rushes the object of discontent, either veering off at the last minute or stopping suddenly to slap its paws against the ground or a tree and loudly huff or chomp its jaws. It may sit, walk stiff-legged, or look away prior to a subsequent charge. "If a black bear signals a charge," says Rogers, "he's generally not going to attack."

Whether the bear ever intended to charge at all, let alone follow through with it, the human may take credit for surviving the encounter at great peril and against all odds (as the teller recalls). "There wouldn't be nearly so many good bear stories if it weren't for the word *if*," says Rogers.

"Black bears use even more restraint than I gave them credit for a few years ago," Rogers said, leaning back in his chair, fingers meshed behind his head. Earlier on, he says, he thought he had to be quick to escape the lunges of captured or denned bears he was approaching. Now he realizes that his safety margin was due in large part to restraint by the bears.

For example: Rogers once knelt about a yard from a ground nest containing a sow and two newborn cubs. He had his camera, as usual, and took a flash photo of the family. Just then he noticed that his focal image was obstructed. Peering over the viewfinder, he saw the female staring at him from the objective side, inches away. Rogers leaped back; the bear, satisfied, returned to her cubs. The photo later depicted a bear, ears flattened, beginning its lunge.

Another: One April, Rogers approached a cave den from which a sow and her cubs were about to emerge. When he was ten feet away the sow lunged to the entrance. She quickly withdrew, and Rogers peered in the hole. She again lunged, but only halfway to the entrance. When Rogers crawled part way in (a habit of his), the bear retreated to the rear of the den, leaving her cubs exposed to him.

From the Smoky Mountains comes the story of a human youngster tormenting a panhandling bear. Eventually running out of patience, the bear

Black bears may make frightening bluff charges against annoying people or other bears. This charging bear was photographed during one of Lynn Rogers' and Gregg Wilker's experiments, when they actually tried to elicit a charge. The bear, although chasing Wilker, avoided touching him and completely ignored Rogers, who was lying on the ground nearby to take this photo. The admonition to never get between a mother bear and her cubs applies more to grizzly bears than to black bears. This is one of the wild bear families that Greg Wilker and Lynn Rogers (pictured) befriend and studied.

took the child's neck in its jaws, pinned him to the ground, then moved off. The boy was left frightened, but without a mark on him. There are hundreds of reports like this one. "The restraint that the powerful black bear normally displayed in these circumstances," wrote Herrero, "always amazes me."

Has Rogers himself ever had what he would call a close call? Well, yes, once, he confesses. Maybe. He was photographing a female and cubs that were somewhat accustomed to people. (I note a possible relationship between bear charges and this bothersome camera habit.) Somehow he startled the cubs; they yelled and leaped for trees. The sow, which had been feeding about twenty-five feet away, whirled and rushed silently with her mouth agape and upper lip raised. Rogers, stumbling backward, tripped. While falling, he hit the bear smartly on the forehead with his camera and kicked her on the chin as he hit the ground. The bear barely noticed his defense. She stood over the fallen photographer and looked up at her cubs. All quiet. She resumed her feeding. Rogers breathed heavily for a minute or two. Unhurt and feeling rather substantiated, he resumed his research.

Black bears, however, do annually injure scores of humans. Although the odds are low, the multiplying multitudes of human-bear interactions each year render even the unlikely exceptions more numerous. The majority of these injuries are minor, however, sometimes but not often requiring stitches. Many are incidental—not intended by the bear involved. Herrero relates a most poetic example of this, in which a "matronly" woman was feeding a black bear, coaxing it to stand close to her. On the way back down to all fours, the bear accidentally caught the woman's blouse with its claws, baring her to the waist and causing very superficial scratches. The woman demanded the bear be killed for this "attack," but the park ranger in charge, thankful for the bear story of a lifetime, refused her request.

A small percentage of black bear attacks result in major injury to humans. Victims of these maulings have sometimes precipitated the attack by injuring the bear first, usually in futile and senseless fashion. Wounded, threatened, or cornered bears are the ones most likely to attack, says Rogers. Shooting a treed adult bear with a pistol, for example, and then cornering the injured animal constitutes what the animal behaviorists refer to as "asking for it." Read Herrero for the real-life examples. We should note that the human victims of even these circumstances often escape with their lives. (I say human victims because the bears are victims too, and less likely to obtain medical assistance afterwards.)

Do black bears really kill people? Yes, of course they do, but very rarely. "Bears attack and kill other bears," writes behaviorist Dale McCullough. "Why should humans expect greater consideration?" Humans attack and kill their fellow men and women, one might add, at a rate over 90,000 times that of black bear manslaughter.

Herrero listed twenty-three human deaths perpetrated by black bears in the past century. One additional incident occurred more recently at an oil drilling station in British Columbia. This brings to twenty-four the number of human lives documented lost to black bears in this century. This in light of the hundreds of thousands of interactions between the two species. For each one of these deaths, approximately seventeen people in North America have died of spiderbites, twenty-five by snakebite, and sixty-seven due to attacks by domestic dogs. Next time you wonder, while erecting your little mountain tent on the ridge at the edge of the timber, whether you've cached your bacon far enough away, remember this: On the whole you are statistically three hundred seventy-four times more likely to be killed by a bolt of lightning than by a black bear. See if you can find that in your park service brochure.

Why do black bears attack humans? Most bluff charges and minor injuries are the results of defensive behavior by bears being fed, crowded, harassed, or petted by humans. Touching a wild bear crosses the behavioral boundary which the bears usually won't cross among themselves.

When threatened, cubs climb the nearest tree. The mother bear may also run to the tree and climb up after her cubs, as this sow is doing.

"Some bears bluff charge people simply to separate the people from their food," notes Rogers, "just as bears chase other bears away from food patches." Offensive charges are otherwise rare, and usually occur between bears over mates or cubs.

One of the most popular fears of black bear encounters is that of encountering a mother with her cubs. This, too, may be a carry-over from the typical and well-known behavior of grizzly females which may charge any perceived threat to their cubs. Sometimes without restraint.

With that in mind, I asked Rogers about the danger of surprising a female black bear with cubs. "Way overblown," he said. I might've expected; he and several other bear biologists regularly tag the ears of young cubs by chasing families and catching the bawling cubs as they climb trees to escape. The sows woof and threaten, sometimes charge to within twenty feet, but generally move off and wait, rejoining their cubs shortly after the ordeal.

Herrero agrees that black bear mothers may bluff ferociously when cubs are endangered, but rarely attack. A few observations suggest that female black bears are more likely to injure a person if the threat to her cubs occurs in close proximity to a number of people, as near a crowd of tourists feeding bears at roadside. Even then, he says, the bears usually will tolerate all but the most extreme harassment.

Why else might a black bear approach a human? Possibly out of simple curiosity. The black bear is highly inquisitive, and the human, after all, is a mighty curious animal. An incident in Aurora, Minnesota, in August 1986, illustrates the point. Petite young Lois Brown was carrying her puppy through the woods near a landfill when she saw a bear running up behind her, making a lot of noise. Lois ran, but fell several times, stopping to pick up the puppy each time. The bear stayed in pursuit but failed to catch them. She ran about a half mile, the bear still behind her, dropped the dog, ran a little further and fell, exhausted. This time she curled into a ball and waited. The bear approached, sniffed her

feet, up her back. Then it backtracked and checked out the pup, but returned to Lois, this time to sniff around her head. And then this bear—which possessed the speed to catch Lois all along, and the strength to injure her or carry the dog off like a morsel—wandered off. Lois hurried home. The dog showed up that evening, wagging its little tail outside a local eatery.

And why would a black bear kill a human? In fact, all of the human deaths and most major injuries caused by black bears have been classed behaviorally as predaceous attacks. In extremely rare cases, certain individual black bears consider humans prey. (Grizzlies have killed twice as many people as black bears but primarily by offensive or defensive procedures, not predaceously.)

Markedly different from aggressive charges, the predaceous black bear attack entails no warning signals, no vocalizations. Predation, after all, is work, specialized work, demanding proper technique: silence and stealth. It occurs primarily during daylight (most fatal grizzly attacks occur at night), with a careful stalk on the part of the bear, often from behind the victim. There are no preliminary or repeated false charges, but rather a quick, quiet, and clean debilitating attack directed toward the victim's head and neck, after which the bear carries the victim away.

What elicits the predaceous attack is still unknown, due in part to the extreme rarity of the behavior. Few causative patterns have surfaced. A number of the attacks, including one in Ontario's Algonquin Park on May 13, 1978, in which three teenagers were killed, involved fishermen. The suggestion arises that the bear was attracted by fish. Yet is appears that few black bears choose fish as food, even when available. Rogers reports that black bears avoid fish and fish parts in Minnesota dumps.

Some, but not all, of the predaceous bears have appeared undernourished. Sudden confrontation does not precipitate this kind of attack. Nor is food conditioning believed to be a regular contributing circumstance. Predaceous attacks occur primarily in rural or backcountry settings and involve black bears which have had little or no association with humans.

On September 14 and 15, 1987, two unprovoked attacks by a black bear in the Boundary Waters Canoe Area scarred a perfect record of over eighteen million visitor days with no bear attack. The bear's behavior during both attacks fit a predatory description and led to their classification as predaceous attacks, even though she was a campground animal, food-conditioned, human habituated, and apparently thin, especially for September. Both men attacked survived. "What we had here," said Lynn Rogers, who helped investigate the incident, "was simply a bear who had lost her sense of judgment." Twenty-seven years earlier, S.C. Whitlock came to a similar conclusion when analyzing the predaceous bear attack on a three-year-old girl in Sault Ste. Marie, Michigan. He, too, could only conclude that the bear involved, aside from being hungry, had an "abnormal mental make-up."

During food shortages bears roam farther and are more likely to come into contact with people, sometimes causing encounters when going after livestock, crops, garbage, or wild foods such as blueberries. "When bears are really hungry," Rogers told me, "they become more aggressive toward food and people. This isn't due to any learning process; it comes naturally." But confrontations in these cases have usually not resulted in predaceous behavior. In interior Alaska in the summer of 1963, hungry bears wandered outside their normal home ranges and into campsites and the rare productive blueberry patch, spawning a record number of nuisance and attack reports. The bears appeared emaciated, irritable, but usually not predaceous toward people. Yet as Rogers himself points out, there were three fatal predaceous attacks that year—an unusually high number.

Some have speculated that the Boundary Waters attacks of 1987 were caused by the hunger of the bear involved, yet just two years earlier Minnesota had suffered the worst bear-food shortage on record. Hundreds of bears from as far away as the Canadian Shield in Ontario wandered south in search of richer soils and better foods. No predaceous behavior was observed.

It may be arguable that abnormal hunger, perhaps coupled with disease or general poor health, can affect a bear's mental make-up in such a way as to render it susceptible to the human predation behavior. The Boundary Waters attack bear had, according to placental scars examined during her autopsy, lost two litters in successive years, suggesting either physical health problems or a hormonal disorder. I think of a story Lynn Rogers told me about a twenty-one-year-old sow who gave birth to two cubs and two months later bit one's head off and smashed the other with a paw. Subject to abnormally fast weight loss, and too undernourished to complete hibernation, she fell out of biochemical balance, urinated in the den and died there two days after killing the cubs. Both the physiology of hibernation and the control of behavior depend in part upon hormonal balances; in an animal with as complex a biochemical cycle as the black bear, then, any relationship between unusual behavior and hormonal imbalance would not be surprising.

Speculation abounds regarding the cause of these unlikely and uncommon predaceous attacks. Running away from a bear elicits the chasing reaction, suggest some. The presence of blood during an aggressive encounter may stimulate predaceous behavior, say others. There is little evidence for either in the case of black bears, says Rogers.

We hear a lot about food conditioning. More human-scented food exists in the backcountry and front-country of bear habitat today; perhaps black bears are beginning to associate humans with the concept of food. Perhaps this leads to more frequent attacks. Doubtful, says Rogers, pointing out that food conditioning does not necessarily predispose black bears to nuisance or predatory behavior. The black bear, he reminds us, can rely upon his nose, with or without training, to detect the palatability of bacon and beans.

We might even wonder whether bears are becoming habituated to the presence of humans in greater numbers than ever in the bush. The more common humans are in the bears' world, the more likely they are to appear as prey, we might hypothesize. Mary Meagher, supervisory wildlife biologist at Yellowstone National Park, told me she feels she is seeing bears becoming habituated to people without food. "There are just too many people in the backcountry," she said, "and the bears are meeting them out there."

True, replies Rogers. But is this leading to a disproportionate number of bear attacks? Is the frequency of bear attacks increasing faster than the number of bear-human encounters? Are we, in other words, teaching more bears to consider humans as prey? Apparently not.

Much like humans, bears have their own personalities, which persist from year to year, as attested to by researchers who watch individual bears quite intimately and those who know them only by number, radio frequency, and daily locus point. This individuality could be the entire explanation for predaceous activity by certain bears. No one knows, but for now the causes and speculations are at best a minor point, interesting to discuss but far overshadowed in any logical consideration by the extreme rarity of the behavior. Based on an estimated population of five hundred thousand black bears in North America and an assumed life term of fifteen years, we may calculate that less than one-thousandth of one percent of all the black bears which have lived in this century are known to have killed a human.

How best to avoid being attacked by a black bear? Much advice exists. I trotted the classic "bear country cautions" past Rogers for his reaction: Never run away from a black bear, lest you elicit the carnivore's chase behavior. "I've always heard this," said Rogers, "but never from anyone who's tested it. Haven't seen it myself."

Always be alert in bear country; watch for sign in berry country; make noise along the trail; keep an eye on your kids. "This is grizzly advice," Rogers told me. "This is silly for black bears. It's rabble-rousing. Why not always be alert in spider country?"

A dominant reaction by the human confronted will likely send a black bear off down the trail. Gary Alt recounts the time a large male stood facing him and abruptly charged. When the bear was twenty-five feet away and closing, Alt let out a loud squawk. The bear turned around in mid-stride and ran off. He looked confused, Alt says. Doug Peacock, famed for his close association with grizzlies, offers similar advice. When tested by a bear, he says, one should assert dominance. "You have to stand up and talk to them."

If surprised by a black bear, then, assume or maintain a dominant posture. Speak to the bear with an assertive voice and calm assurance. If it is cornered, allow escape.

According to Barrie Gilbert's investigations in Yosemite, fear is the human behavior most likely to precede black bear aggression. The second most likely is what he calls "visual neutrality and approach"—the typical pattern of a wildlife photographer moving in for one more, one final close-up. Mild human aggression precedes the fewest black bear charges. People generally respond to bear aggression with fear or performed neutrality, says Gilbert, the precise responses which reinforce nuisance bear approaches by rewarding them with less interference. "Perhaps people should not act too unaggressive with problem black bears," he wrote, "but respond with mild forms of human aggression that do not bring the species too close together."

What about the rare and unlikely case in which a female confronts you in the protection of her cubs? Best to keep talking, slowly back away, and remove yourself as a threat, according to Herrero. Maybe, says Rogers, but she very well may want to get to her cubs or to the tree they climbed. Best then to get quickly out of the way so she can redirect her attention from you to the cubs. Resist "passively" writes Herrero, and play dead if the sow attaches

Mailmen have used capsaicin spray on dogs for over twenty years. The repellent is similarly effective on black bears. When five-year-old Kelly Rogers sprayed this bear in the eyes, it ran away. The repellent irritates the bear's eyes but is not harmful. A disturbing and threatening sound to a mother bear is the rustling noise of a tree being climbed; it can mean frightened cubs are climbing to escape danger or that an intruding bear is climbing to catch her cubs. When Lynn Rogers climbed this tree, which one of his study bears had been using as a refuge for her cubs, she came running from a hundred yards away to climb up after him. She only stopped climbing after she sniffed his foot and heard his familiar voice, assuring her that he was not a bear.

herself to you in the defense of her cubs.

More good advice: When camping in bear country, check your site for previous campers' garbage and signs of bear visitation so you'll know what to expect. Most likely, a challenging bear is after your food. Keep your campsite clean. At home or cabin in bear country, keep your garbage disposed and secure.

Particularly in the East, black bears will run to avoid trouble, even if willing at first to approach a human or his camp. "Rattle the fry pans together," my friend John Lanier, a U.S. Forest Service biologist with the cumbersome physique and nature of a dominant old boar, advises his backcountry staff. "And if that doesn't work, ding a boot at them." Sound advice so far, he reports.

If that doesn't work, throw rocks or spray the bear with a repellant. Several are now available. Rogers, who carried mail for years prior to his graduate schooling, has tested a dog spray, capsaicin, on dump bears and found it effective. A chemical agent isolated from Cayenne peppers, capsaicin is a powerful irritant of sensory nerve endings, but engenders no blisters or injury and causes no lasting harm. Aim for the eyes, he says. It has no effect otherwise. It may be the best-known tool for stopping a bear from eating your food, but to date no one has tested it on a "highly motivated" or predaceous bear.

If all else fails, as a last resort surrender you food. Back off calmly, with your organ systems intact. Better to go hungry for a few days.

And in the exceedingly rare case of attack by a silent, stalking, predaceous black bear—never, never, never play dead. Fight with any weapon you can find. Go for the nose with something meaningful. Survivors of these attacks have driven the bears away using boots, rocks, an ax, canoe paddles, branches, and their own fists.

Rogers was rummaging around behind piles of data and official-looking documents, trying to find a video he had put together on the subject of black bear charges. I looked out the large window in the west wall of his office toward the river. Bears mosey by here occasionally. In the summer of 1984, Rogers began leaving scraps of beef fat outside this window. Natural food was scarce, and Rogers was trying to keep his local objects of study from raiding the public campground a few hundred yards upriver. The technique worked. The bears walked right past the campground and made hundreds of visits of Rogers' office.

It was the beginning of real trust between the bears and Rogers. For Rogers, 1984 and 1985 were the beginnings of a new era of one-on-one bear study. His stated goal was a better understanding of bear behavior and communication to help campers and hikers. His unstated goal was a closeup study like he had done in years past with moose and white-tailed deer, like Dian Fossey had done with gorillas, to provide forest managers with the detailed knowledge they need to maintain bear habitat in the face of increasing human demands upon forest resources.

"I began walking with them in the yard and following them into the forest," said Rogers. "But some of the bears weren't too sure about the forest part of this at first. Little Brownie, a yearling male, would sleep near me in the yard but was nervous about being followed in the woods. Female 401, a radio-collared two-year-old, would run ahead of me in the forest for up to two hours on windy days before I could see her. Finally she would move downwind, smell me, and eventually come. She was most concerned about other bears, and gusty winds make the forest sound like bears are rustling all around. When she would finally come, she would usually still be so nervous that she would blow and lunge toward me before making her final approach, a simple show of nervousness like a gorilla's chest-thumping display."

"She was the first bear I spent very much time with at night. The first time was a breezy June evening during mating season. She came to the lab and was soon joined by Maurice, a young adult male that had appeared only a few days earlier but already

Black bear copulation takes place in spring, and males and females may both mate with several partners. Because only one egg may be fertilized per copulation, black bear litters are usually comprised of cubs fathered by more than a single male, which enhances the genetic diversity of bear populations.

was fairly accepting of people. The two wrestled and played and drifted off into the forest. I followed. The bears didn't seem to mind my coming, but it soon became too dark to see them as anything more than patches of blackness moving inaudibly over the damp moss and leaves. They disappeared into the shadows and then materialized right next to me, at times, to glide past and resume their playing and wrestling. The sudden appearances were disconcerting but at the same time reassuring. I felt at great disadvantage without a flashlight, but the bears proved to be as non-threatening by night as they had been by day.

"I was beginning to learn things I could only wonder about in my previous eighteen years of bear research. Bears in the early stages of accepting me showed their nervous and defensive side. Bears that fully accepted me showed their relaxed side as they went about making a living in the forest. They showed how they responded to insects, weather, foods, and danger. They paid more attention to tiny unidentified sounds in the distance than they did to me. I was not a threat or a protector, not a competitor or a food-giver. The bears used the same vocalizations and body language toward me that they used with each other, but I was not part of their hierarchy and not involved in their disputes or play. The one time a bear playfully bit my foot while I was lying down, I yelled. The bear ran and never tried to play with me again. But just as I had not understood his play, the bears did not understand petting. They moved away or slapped or nipped defensively. I quit trying to pet them. I seemed to be inconsequential to the bears. When 401 and Maurice mated, they let me crawl into their dense balsam fir thicket and break away branches within two feet of their faces for a picture. When a mother with cubs detected a bear in the forest ahead, she stiffened beside me with ears and eyes focused ahead. Suddenly she rushed forward, chasing a young female that she and I both recognized as her independent two-year-old daughter that shared her territory. The chase ended when the daughter slipped going up a rock outcrop

with the mother so close she almost ran into her. The mother did no more than slap the ground behind the daughter as if to say "Get going!" Other mothers I was with showed similar tolerance to their independent offspring, but it was a different story when female 812 discovered a strange young male in her territory. She chased him up a tree, bit him, threw him out, slid down, and went after him again. Yet, I was essentially ignored."

In the fall of 1985, Rogers hired a part-time field assistant, Greg Wilker, a perceptive nineteen-year-old with the common sense of a country upbringing and the patience of a hunter. Greg's first close contact with bears came on his first morning at work. He arrived early and found Lynn with 401, a bear Greg would come to know well. Greg had an open mind, a necessity in work that goes against much of what a person believes about black bears. Under Rogers' tutelage, Greg soon began to interpret bear aggression in terms of the bears' fears rather than his own fears. Within a month, Greg got his first lone assignment. Lynn asked, "I haven't seen 401 for a couple days. Would you be willing to home in on her radio signal and see if she's making a den?"

"Why not?"

He did. She was, and she didn't run away. She climbed several yards up a small tree in mild protest, returned to the ground, and approached Greg. Surprised, Greg climbed several yards up a tree himself. The bear stood up, sniffed Greg's feet, returned to the den, and lay down. Greg climbed down, heart pounding with excitement, ready for more lone assignments.

Lynn and Greg took turns visiting 401 at her den that fall and kept track of her the following spring by walking in on her radio signal. She accepted Greg into her circle of fully acceptable humans. One day, Greg reported to Rogers that he had followed her closely for ten hours straight. Rogers asked, "Do you think you could stay with her longer? Say, for twenty-four hours?" "Probably," said Greg. "And record everything she does, every bite she eats, every rock she turns over?" Rogers

inquired. "Why not?" said Greg. And he did.

What Rogers calls "taming down" a bear is not a taming process. Rather, it corresponds to the removal of one major variable in interpreting how a bear behaves on its landscape. That variable being how the bear reacts to its alien observer. By removing this uncertainty, Rogers can better see, more thoroughly understand, the more subtle and secretive side of a black bear's lifestyle. The bears, for their part, go along with the charade, maintaining their natural patterns, ignoring the pesky biologist.

Thus Rogers shifted the focus of his studies and the ramparts of black bear research. What had started sixteen years earlier as the typical black bear population study now became an intensive investigation into habitat use by bears.

In addition to the twenty-four hour work, Rogers and Wilker have been further investigating black bear restraint behavior. Wilker has experimentally teased various bears he knows while Rogers lies behind Greg, filming reactions. Once, when Wilker successfully elicited a charge, he tripped while "escaping" and fell. The bear in pursuit literally fell over herself to avoid touching him. "There was no way she wanted to make contact," says Rogers, whom the bear had nearly run over in the process.

He'd like to pursue the question of bear aggression even further and try facing down a known predaceous bear. "So far, most victims have run away or played dead at some point in the encounter, and that's when they were injured," he told me. "Do you really expect to pull that off?" I asked him. He shook his head disappointedly, "No," he said. "You just can't find a predaceous bear."

So, once and for all, how dangerous is the black bear? Whom do we ask? The bears still aren't talking. We can't trust the purveyors of pulp stories, and certainly not the paranoid park service brochures. The top investigators and biologist agree in principle but not in degree. So who then?

Taped (with pride) to a wall of Lynn Rogers' office hangs a yellowed newspaper headline, decapitated from the body of an article long since misplaced. It reads:

THE BEARMAN KNOWETH
We'll ask him.

"I'm much more impressed by the black bear's restraint than by its ferocity," Rogers says. "It's tough to convince people that what they want to believe is a ferocious animal, isn't."

And how about Wilker? He's a bear man too. How safe and certain does he feel, prowling the dark bush after one of these powerful, hungry opportunists? "Well," he says, "I feel a lot more comfortable walking with the bears out there than I would walking downtown in some city."

Are the bears perfectly predictable then? No, not perfectly, says Rogers. "Don't you think you might play out your odds one of these days?" I ask him. He smiles. "My chances of meeting the rare predaceous bear are too slim to worry about. And I've never seen a hungry bear that I couldn't get rid of with a squirt of capsaicin. I might add that I am a cautious person by nature; I don't take unnecessary chances. I've learned in twenty-two years of study that black bears are not a major danger."

In truth, black bears are not terrifying creatures, but neither are we perfectly safe among them. And let's hope it never comes to that. So what kind of picture are we left with? Why, the same story we are learning about our environment and the earth itself. We needn't fear the black bear, but rather must respect it and try to better understand it.

As usual, danger—natural danger—isn't half as bad as it's cracked up to be. The true thrill of the wilderness today lies in the challenge of understanding it. And those who live and die there, as we once did.

Bears that visit the North Central Forest Experiment Station in northeastern Minnesota become accustomed to walking onto a scale for a small food reward.

CHAPTER 4

THE GREAT AMERICAN BEAR

"What we seem to want is a statistically homogenized picture of a species, when we really need to look at bears as dynamic, living mechanisms."
— Dr. Barrie Gilbert

Thus far in its evolution the black bear remains an adaptable species, highly variable in behavior, function, and physique. Quite difficult to adequately portray.

What follows, then, is not intended to summarize or summarily describe the black bear. Based on research and field observations from throughout North America, it is not designed to delineate what *Ursus americanus* is, but to approach what it might be, according to reality and Dr. Gilbert's terms. Think of it as an incomplete set of blazes along a trail, rough and obscure, through a dark forest.

THE BLACK BEAR

Phylogenetic Affiliation

Kingdom Animalia, phylum Cordata (contains a backbone), class Mammalia, order Carnivora, family Ursidae, genus and species, *Ursus americanus*. Close relatives include *Ursus arctos*, the grizzly and brown bears, and *Ursus maritimus*, the polar bear, and *Selenarctos thibetanus*, the Asiatic black bear. Four other species of bears live today, if you count the giant panda. The spectacled bear of South America, *Tremarctos aunatus*, is the only other bear is the western hemisphere and the only one living in the southern hemisphere.

Origins

The first fossil evidence of bears appears during the Miocene epoch, from early predatory tree-climbing stock related to the canids. Adapted to and comfortable in the forest biome since its beginnings, the black bear's physiology and lifestyle have been affected heavily and in unique fashion by forest and winter seasons since the Pleistocene. The first likeness of the black bear appeared in North America about five hundred thousand years ago—five times longer ago than the appearance here of grizzlies, and one thousand times longer ago than human explorers from Europe.

Distribution

The American black bear has restricted itself to the continent of its birth. Black bears are found wherever sufficient tree cover remains, which today means parts of a maximum of forty of the forty-nine states in which it once ranged. All Canadian provinces and as few as twenty-three to as many as twenty-eight states retain what might be considered viable populations. An unknown but tiny number survive in the mountains of northern Mexico, threatened by deforestation and an ever-expanding human population. Loss of forest habitat to development and agriculture is not the only reason for the reduction in black bear distribution. Fragmentation of habitat by roads and corridors of development can damage a forest's capacity to support black bears.

In eastern North America the black bear is a denizen of forest and swamp; in the West, of the mountains. Wherever found, it prefers areas that contain the thickest vegetational cover. Overall distribution includes most of Canada and Alaska, the mountainous West Coast, the Rocky Mountains southward into northern Mexico, the Appalachians southward to northern Georgia, forest fragments in Florida and the Gulf Coast through Texas, and a remote population center around northeastern Arkansas. The northern boundary of black bear distribution generally traces the northern extent of the forest itself. Since 1944, however, an increasing number of black bears have been killed or observed out on the barren grounds east and west of Hudson Bay. More recently, black bears have been observed ranging into the subalpine meadowlands of Yosemite National Park. This may attest to the black bear's range of adaptability as well as the regional disappearance of its chief competing species, the grizzly. Grizzlies are gone from Yosemite, and the

Black bears require water for cooling and drinking, although berries can supply sufficient dietary water needs in season.

barren ground grizzly west of Hudson Bay has suffered a great reduction in numbers. Grizzlies do not live east of Hudson Bay, although they probably once did, according to evidence collected from early fur trader and explorer reports by C. S. Elton in 1954 and corroborated when C. R. Harrington discovered a grizzly cranium in a cave on the Gaspe Peninsula in 1978.

Physical Specifications

Smallest of the North American bears, the black bear measures five to six feet from head to tail and two to three feet high at the withers. Its lack of a shoulder hump and its prominent ears are the best field marks to differentiate it from the grizzly. Weights are extremely variable among individuals, habitats, seasons, and annual food availability. Adult males reach maximum size by age twelve and are one and a half to two times the size of adult females, which peak in their sixth year, according to Rogers' Minnesota data. Adult males usually range between 150 and 550 pounds, females 90 to 300, except for the occasional outsized individual. Examples: Dave Graber found adult females in Yosemite to average 191 pounds, and adults males 312. In a recent Massachusetts study Ken Elowe calculated averages of 139 and 229 pounds for adult females and males, respectively. Gary Alt found the average fall weight of mature males to be 486 pounds in Pennsylvania, home of the world's best black bear habitat. Bears there are larger by sex and age class than Yellowstone grizzlies. Lynn Rogers once trapped a 611-pound bear he discovered foraging in a dump in northeastern Minnesota. In *Outdoor Life* magazine, Ben East reported a black bear shot by Otto Hedbany in Glidden, Wisconsin, which dressed out at 665 pounds, and which he calculated may have weighed 720 alive. (By rule of thumb, field dressing removes ten to twenty percent of a bear's body weight. The bigger the bear, the lower the percentage.) In 1986 a 723-pound male was registered at a Pennsylvania hunter check station. An 802-pound bear was reported taken in Wisconsin in 1885. An 803-pound bear was weighed and released at a dump by Paul Paqnet in Manitoba on September 9, 1987.

That bear had gained 373 pounds in seventy-five days since an earlier capture when it weighed 430 pounds, on June 25, 1987. And Earnest Thompson Seton himself listed the largest I have come across in the literature, an alleged 900-pound cattle killer removed for the good of Arizona by officials of the U.S. Biological Survey in 1921. One might suspect an upward bias in this estimate, however. The only people likely to underestimate a bear's weight are the wildlife biologist calculating his dosage of immobilatory drug and the illicit trader, buying by the pound.

Standard black bear features include forty-two teeth, six mammae, two brown eyes, and a tail—short, often concealed. In eastern North America the typical *Ursus americanus* is black with a lighter brown muzzle, Roman nose, and often a small tuft or patch of white hair on the chest. Brown color phases—chocolate through red and cinnamon to blond—occur more commonly in the West, where they may serve as protective coloration (mimicking the grizzly bear) or to absorb less solar heat under more-open forest cover. Well adapted to cool temperatures and forest shade, bears are susceptible to overheating during the warm seasons, and black fur absorbs heat most readily. Melanin, the dark pigment in the fur, may serve as well to harden the bear's coat against the abrasion of the thicker cover in the East. Alt recently reported less than one percent brown-phase bears in Pennsylvania, while a study in southwestern Colorado reported more than eighty percent brown. In Minnesota, which was post-glacial open country as recently as four thousand years ago, Rogers sees brown fur on one of every twenty or thirty bears, or one of every ten sometime during its life. Genetically inherited, color may change on an individual from one year to the next. Parents which are or once were brown are more likely to have brown cubs which retain the color. Litters may be mixed.

Near Glacier Bay in southeastern Alaska and

*Compared with black bears, brown bears (**Ursus arctos**) and grizzly bears (**Ursus arctos horribilis**) have stubbier ears, a larger shoulder hump, and longer claws. No grizzly or brown bears live east of the Great Plains. Black bear litters may include cubs of both black and brown color phases. Black fur is the rule in eastern forests. Brown is more common in open areas of the West. Five to ten percent of black bears in forests along the eastern edge of the Great Plains are of the brown phase, like the two in this Minnesota black bear family.*

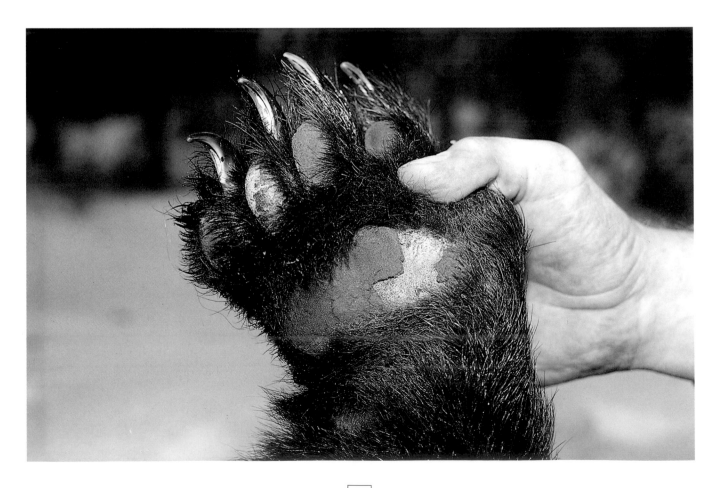

nearby Canada you may find a blue or blue-gray color phase known as the "glacier bear." And restricted mostly to a few islands along the coast of British Columbia is the Kermode bear, an all-white color phase—with brown eyes, not the pigmentless pink of albinism—which is now rare. Both phases occur infrequently in populations which are predominantly black.

Black bears molt and grow a new coat each summer. The new coat remains prime through the inactivity of winter and into May.

Testicles are stored out of the way in the abdomen from late summer until the following spring. Rogers believes this phenomenon explains many stories about "big ol' sows" treed by hunters in the fall.

Bear tracks show five toes and may exhibit claw marks. In a walking pace the hind foot just overreaches the front. Black bear tracks may show shorter claws, better separated toe pads, and more fur between toe pads and sole, than grizzly tracks. On a typical grizzly track you can draw a straight line separating the toe marks from the pad; on a black bear track this line would have to be curved. The big toe is attached to the outside of the bear's foot.

Black bears shed the dead outer skin of their foot pads during winter dormancy. The new underlying skin is soft and sensitive at first, and the bears tend to lick these areas during the shedding process. Native Americans who observed this believed that bears provided for their winter nourishment by licking or sucking their paws after saturating them with berry juices through the summer. One Abenaki legend proposed that bears sucked body fat out through the soles of their feet for survival. Hallowell, in his treatise on bear ceremonialism, found a rough correlation between the distribution of this basic belief and the occurrence of the bear cult itself.

Digestive Tract

The gastro-intestinal tract of this animal measures longer in respect to body size than that of true carnivores—an adaptation that minimizes the need for protracted chewing. Seeds and husks are routed exteriorly according to the usual process.

General Disposition

Contrary to popular opinion, the black bear is a shy, retiring animal. It possesses less desire to see humans than most humans possess to see the bear. The black bear is inclined to escape—not attack, nor even bluff—a human presence.

From all indications, the black bear is a happy animal when unmolested, with a strong purpose in life (feeding) and plenty of time to pursue it.

Senses

The black bear's sense of smell may be most acute. They possess one hundred times the area of sensitive olfactory membranes as that found in humans, and have been followed more than a mile through dense woods in a straightaway approach to a carcass of which they had no former knowledge. They are able to locate rich patches of mast in much the same fashion, and sniff out tiny insects in large rotting logs. The presence of a vestigial vomeronasal (Jacobson's) organ, sensitive to airborne chemical gradients, in the roof of the mouth enhances olfaction.

"Most of the bears I've encountered were already looking at me when I saw them," writes veteran bear hunter Bob Bell, "even when the wind—and thus their acute sense of smell—was not a factor." The black bear's hearing is more sensitive than that of a human, and its visual acuity may be superior to former expectations. It can discriminate among colors and hues; in the Smokies, panhandling bears now recognize park rangers from a distance by both uniform and vehicle.

Vocal Repertoire

Depending upon age and its current disposition, the black bear may emit any of a variety of bawls, hums, woofs, huffs, chomps, moans, blows, snorts, gurgles, grunts, and the occasional growl. All are described elsewhere.

Some black bears change color. This yearling male shed his beautiful light golden fur and molted into rich dark chocolate fur. The last fur to molt is typically along the back midline. In the process of molting this cub is losing the last of its black guard hairs and will so lose the brown, woolly underfur that it needed in spring. The cub's new summer coat came in black, as is usual where it lived on Grandfather Mountain in North Carolina. In late summer and fall, it again grew underfur in preparation for winter. Bears shed their calloused foot pads during the last half of hibernation and may lick their tender feet in the den. A myth once believed by people throughout the northern hemisphere is that bears survive over winter by licking their feet to obtain the essence of berries that were crushed into them the previous year.

Habits

The black bear is a full-time professional food consumer. He lives to eat, as the saying goes, and eats to live. Except for his winter sleep and those few complicated weeks around late June, he spends his waking hours occupied with nutrient input. The voyageurs had a name for black bears—*Cochons de bois*, "pigs of the woods." George Laycock once described the bear as an animal of "perpetual hunger." And why not? Any creature of this bulk that needs to lay down enough fat in two seasons, by pushing vegetable matter through its short gut, to sleep away half the year or more had better be serious about his feed. As much as the forest shaped the bear and the Pleistocene designed its physiology, the distribution and supply of foods dictates the individual bear's daily schedule and behavior.

What does the black bear eat? Anything it can find, goes the old saw, implying that slitting open a bear, shark-like, one might find old boots, three-pound tins of Spam, sections of anchor chain. This is not accurate. While black bears are highly omnivorous and able to take advantage of a wide variety of food items and types, they also appear to be selective feeders most of the time. Lynn Rogers has seen a black bear ignore a tub of beef suet and travel twenty-two miles cross country to pick nuts off the ground under a small stand of hardwoods. Bears in Yellowstone have shunned raw bacon and fresh eggs for richer delicacies, including Colgate toothpaste, worn sneakers, and Coleman fuel lapped from the ground after perforating a lantern's reservoir with those handy canines.

Yet bears almost always select natural foods over man-made, and generally seek out the most digestible and highly nutritional foods in season. Usually these include vegetables and fruits. These plant foods vary extremely among habitats and geography, and from year to year with climatic variation.

In spring, before the berries ripen, black bears eat great quantities of tender young grass shoots and newly emerging forest plants (difficult to digest, but easier when young than after hardening into cellulose), buds, skunk cabbage, greenbriar berries in the South, ants and other insects, catkins and young leaves. The latter are harvested by drawing a stem through the diastema—the open space remaining between canines and molars in the bear's jaw where premolars are not fully formed—stripping off the leaves and buds. Carrion of winter-killed ungulates (deer, elk, moose, cattle) may be eaten, if available. In spring black bears also prey on moose calves and fawns. Other animal foods may include but are not limited to snails, centipedes, crayfish, bees, larval and adult yellowjackets, frogs, woodchucks, jumping mice, cottontails, and birds' eggs. Claw marks on large poplar trees in an area of the Peace River in Alberta led to speculation that a black bear had learned to deprecate hawk nests. In Massachusetts, biologist Ken Elowe watched a black bear spring delicately on a woodcock and eat it. In a forest opening he observed another bear stuffing a little brown bird, highly animated, into its maw.

Spring is the critical time for bear survival, and autumn is the time to lay on fat reserves for metabolism during the crucial period after bears come out of hibernation. Breeding is relegated to the spring-autumn interim, generally in June and early July. Males wander most this time of year, and tolerate each other least. They search out females, in territories which their ranges overlap, by scent; during a short estrus, females perfume their trails with odiferous urine and may consort with one or more males, one at a time. Cubs of a single litter may have different fathers. Of copulation, T. H. White's translation of a twelfth century bestiary erroneously notes that bears use the usual human position; the *History of Four-Footed Beasts* (another bestiary) says correctly that they take a long time "in that act."

Breeding ends and bear summer begins when the berries ripen. Until this time many black bears continue to lose weight, the residue of their winter fat, if any, subsidizing spring metabolism. Now the carbohydrate-rich mast becomes available, soft mast first: blueberries, huckleberries, juneberries,

Eating fruits such as these hawthorne berries provides bears only carbohydrates. Vegetation, nuts, and insects are their main sources of protein and fat, although carbohydrates ingested in sufficient quantities may also be converted to fat. The black bear's sensitive ears and nose allow it to hear and smell potential danger in dense vegetation where visibility is limited. Black bears usually prefer nuts and berries over campground fare, but when wild crops fail, bears are almost as quick as chipmunks to overcome their fear of people.

pin cherries, black cherries, chokecherries, poke-berries, blackberries, sarsaparilla berries, squawroot fruits, raspberries, dewberries, and strawberries, to name a few.

Late summer through autumn is nut season—hard mast, the most concentrated and digestible energy. In hardwood areas of North America bears seek out acorns, beechnuts, hickory nuts, hazelnuts, and once—but no longer—American chestnuts. Chestnuts were the staple and most reliable autumn black bear food throughout the Appalachians until the induced blight annihilated them in the 1940s. In the coniferous western high country, hard mast is comprised of whitebark pine nut alone. Lacking these, black bears of the high country resort to green riparian vegetation and insects—social ants, hornets, and yellow jackets. In Florida where developers appear more indulgent of tropical trees than oak stands, bears turn to needle palm, palmetto, and tupelo berries in autumn, and chew out cabbage palm hearts in April.

The black bear has a few advantages over those species with which it competes for mast. It can bite open the shell of a hickory nut that no deer or turkey could crack, and climb to the crop before it falls to the availability of deer or coyote. Squirrels may harvest the nuts a black bear covets, but they usually bury most of them in ground middens which bears sniff out and plunder. The middens of ground squirrels may contain starchy roots and tubers, and particularly in the fall black bears may hunt for them or dig their own potatoes. (The bear potato, *Arisaemia triphyllum*, was named by Native Americans who discovered them by following the bears.

Theory and Paradox

Here is a creature that can weigh a quarter ton or more, hang by its teeth, and haul down a fully grown Rocky Mountain bull elk in deep snow, but which prefers to climb trees to escape danger, and teases hazelnuts, one by one, from the forest litter. A predator by formal definition, a carnivore by taxonomic rank, it has evolved further away from carnivorous traditions than man himself.

Due to this choice of foods—a choice made, in the evolutionary sense, twenty-five million years ago and which first made the bear line distinct—the black bear's entire ecology, including breeding, productivity, survival, population density, even social organization, is a function of the annual distribution and abundance of tiny fruits and nuts. The production of these foods is controlled and delimited in part by the same cold season which shaped bear physiology.

While the wolf and cougar continue to encourage the fleetness of the deer, the black bear makes its ecological signature by cycling the seeds of favorite fruits through its entrails (a treatment which enhances the germination process) and sowing them on the forest floor. That which is selectively chosen for food is thus selectively encouraged to regenerate by the most conservative and cost effective agricultural technique ever invented.

Productivity

Litters of from one to four cubs are common. In western North America and much of Canada the mode is two cubs; in the East, three. Litters of up to six are observed in Pennsylvania.

In Minnesota, Lynn Rogers has found that litters of three generally contribute the maximum population recruitment by weaning age. Larger litters suffer higher mortality.

First litters are frequently one or two cubs born to sows of from three to eight years of age; the better the habitat, the younger the new mothers. In Pennsylvania first litters contain two or three cubs, and females may breed at two and one half years of age. In marginal habitat, few sows bear their first litters in years after food shortages.

Subsequent litters are dropped every two to four years, more frequently when the food is better. Rogers has found higher productivity among Minnesota sows which have garbage dumps within their home ranges.

Bears wipe bumblebees or hornets off their muzzles but otherwise seem to ignore the attacking insects until the bears have obtained the mass of larvae at the heart of a colony. Then they move on quickly, usually pausing after a few feet to shake dozens of attackers off their protective fur as if they were shaking off water. Although few mammals and birds eat tent caterpillars, black bears eat them by the thousands, despite the caterpillars' protective hairs.

Social Organization

The individual black bear prefers to spend much of its life alone, usually within a stable perimeter, hiding from or turning away its conspecifics as appropriate. It has no need for group protection from other species. Its population is well dispersed, singly and in low density across the forest landscape, in proportion to its scattered foods.

Despite a solitary nature, especially in adult males, a more intensive look at black bears reveals a well-developed social web. The black bear selects options from a highly adaptable social behavior repertoire, which can range from conspecific aggression through subtle mutual avoidance to outright affinity for play partners where food is abundant. Females care diligently for their cubs, usually for one full year and the following spring. Family break-up occurs when the yearlings are about seventeen months old, and even then the young remain within their mother's territory, though apart from her. In productive situations in which females breed in alternate years, they spend seventeen months with their cubs and portions of the ensuing month associating with males, leaving only six months of every two years, or one-fourth of their adult life, in solitude.

Females are territorial; each has a distinct area of land which is home, although she might leave it for a time in late summer or fall to check out feeding conditions miles away. Rogers found mothers showing their cubs feeding areas up to sixty miles away before leading them back home to a den. Cubs remembered the best of those places and returned to them as adults. But the mother's territory is the primary living area for the mother and her offspring from a succession of litters. She marks it with a steady drip of urine as she forages about each day. Her territory is respected by neighboring females and overlaps little with theirs except in small areas of food concentration such as garbage dumps and rich berry patches. While the same general area is used year after year, the exact parcels and amount of land change with seasons and through time.

Findings of a recent study in the southern Appalachians suggest that sows' territories overlap more in areas of high habitat productivity. This overlap may tend to mask female territoriality, particularly in studies depending upon remote telemetric location of study bears.

In Minnesota, Rogers has witnessed "vigorous chases" and fighting among females aggressively defending their territories. One female even killed another in a small area of territory overlap. Under most circumstances, avoidance is the rule, but for reasons unknown, some trespasses occur without challenges, especially late in the year when territoriality seems to relax temporarily as bears check out distant feeding sites.

Young and Ruff, in Alberta, and Jonkel and Cowan, in Montana, found evidence of female territoriality, surmised in part from the small amount of overlap among adult sow home ranges. And if territoriality is a function of habitat quality and food availability, then we can expect variations of its evidence and expression among different kinds of habitat and from one year to the next.

Male offspring voluntarily disperse from their maternal territories between the ages of one and four. They may travel over one hundred miles in search of available range—a piece of land which rival adult males allow them, but which has enough food and some opportunity for nuptial affairs. Relatively little is known about male dispersal. Females are the more critical element of population growth and maintenance, and few researchers relish the prospect of tracking a wandering adolescent boar far beyond transmitter range and across political boundaries. Female sub-adults are allowed to take over a portion of the maternal territory, small at first but growing with the needs of the daughter. As these filial territories grow, it is the bear mother who gives ground, expanding her freehold elsewhere and shifting its core area if necessary.

Adult males are not territorial, though they practice a polite mutual avoidance among other males whose home ranges their own may greatly

Black bear litters average two cubs in western North America and three cubs in the East. A sow's first litter, however, is usually one cub less than the norm. Territorial females may watch, chase, or flee from intruders. Territorial enforcement depends upon the sex and age of the intruder, whether or not the bears are kin, the presence of cubs, food supply, and the personality and hormonal status of the individual. Where food is abundant, bears may choose partners to travel and wrestle with. These unrelated males, three and seven years of age, spent many hours together. Young well-fed males are most likely to find play partners; territorial females are least likely.

overlap. Males' ranges tend to overlap females' territories, but the bruins tend to avoid the core areas of these territories. In Minnesota, Rogers found that one male's range may overlap those of two others as well as the territories of seven to fifteen females.

Female territories, basic units of land large enough to contain sufficient food in an average year to provide for the female and cubs, are smaller than male ranges, the sizes of which function to provide multiple breeding potential. Rogers found females' territories in northeastern Minnesota to average two to four miles in diameter, about three and one-half square miles in area. Males covered ranges of from seven to ten miles across or larger, sometimes hundreds of square miles, areas simply too large to patrol and defend as exclusive territories. In Pennsylvania, female territories average nearly fifteen square miles, males' about sixty. Territory and home range sizes vary with food supply and habitat quality. In northern Maine and New Hampshire, adult females range across about ten square miles each. Young New Hampshire females covered only two or three square miles of their mothers' ranges. Males covered from fifteen to over seventy square miles.

Female home ranges are more stable from year to year, changing little except to accommodate the growth of their daughters' territories within. Male home ranges are less stable, perhaps in part due to the annual shift in obliging females.

Social organization, like everything else in black bear existence, is determined by the distribution, abundance, and reliability of food. Since a berry crop can vary one hundred fold (10,000 percent) from one year to the next, plasticity is the rule. If food is extremely abundant, bears need not protect it so diligently. If food becomes extremely scarce, there may be too little to protect on the territories and bears may wander in search. In either extreme, territoriality might be expected to break down, allow more overlap, and possibly disappear. At such times, or where food is clumped, as in garbage dumps, bears may cast off territoriality— even for a few hours at a time—and adopt a system of dominance hierarchy which allows them to feed in close proximity to one another.

Seasonal ranges for both sexes are likely to be different and smaller than the total annual range. As Gary Alt pointed out to me, the winter home range for most bears is a single locus point on the map, about ten square feet on or under the forest floor. Largest seasonal ranges usually coincide with the breeding season. Families increase their working area as young cubs gain mobility through their first summer. Females with cubs generally cover more country—to find more food—than lone females in a given habitat and year.

Mortality

A black bear may live thirty years or more in captivity. Wild bears able to avoid roads and hunters may survive more than twenty. A twenty-year-old bear in the woods is an old bear, though females of that age may still be reproductively successful.

Adult bears die most commonly due to hunting mortality (accounting for over ninety percent of Minnesota black bear mortality, for example). Other human causes include roadkills, railroad kills, electrocution by powerlines, and the disturbance of winter dens. The adult black bear is virtually immune to predation, though wolves, grizzly bears, and large black bears infrequently prove capable of the task. Cubs are taken by the species noted above, and, primarily in Canada, by lynx.

Starvation is uncommon among adult bears. Among cubs and yearlings, starvation may cause over fifty percent mortality during prolonged periods of food shortages. Starvation usually kills within two months of emergence from the den. Cubs may also succumb to abandonment, den flooding, and falling from trees. Larger litters suffer greater mortality. Under rare and extreme circumstances, cannibalism of young by adult black bears may be significant. Deaths of adolescents are common during dispersal to new living areas.

Intelligence

The myth of the black bear as a bumbling

Young males voluntarily disperse from their mother's territory before mating. Once outside that territory, they are often kept on the move by hostile males and territorial females. Males cover areas too large to defend as territories. Their ranges overlap, and they fight over the females, seven to fifteen living within the range of each mature male. Territorial females are alert to sounds that could be made by an intruding bear.

fool is perpetrated by Americans who have left out containers of bear bait (ham and swiss, freeze-dried chop suey, leftover steak bones, and toothpaste) in bear country, and then suffered the moral indignation of being robbed. The bears, frightened by sudden commotion and hollering and blinded by headlight beams when discovered in their pillaging, stumble through tiers of garbage cans and vari-colored tents in crowded campgrounds, driven off by the new experts in animal behavior.

Real woodsmen and woodswomen know that a bear is intelligent and most agile in his native haunts. Around the fire circles of the Abenaki the black bear had a reputation for looking wise, not wholly undeserved. What other animal lives in peaceful, solitary manner and allows the adolescent males to move out at puberty? "I've seen people doing stupider things than bears," said a veteran conservation officer in northern New Hampshire. And he has the stories to prove it.

Intelligence may be defined as the ability to reason, understand, and learn. Charles Jonkel described bears in *Big Game of North America* as:

". . . highly evolved, intelligent mammals with both genetic and 'culturally inherited' or learned abilities to utilize the resources in their environments, adapt to new ranges, or cope with environmental changes. "

He found in black bears in particular "remarkable capabilities to cope with habitat changes brought about by man."

The bear has a unique brain among carnivores, the largest relative to body length, and one which contains several features similar to a primate brain, including structures which closely resemble the primate temporal lobe. The temporal lobe is believed to integrate the complex sequences of behavior and memory. Behavioral studies indicate that black bears can combine color discrimination with the performance of tasks, and learn to do this faster than chimps. Adaptability, stresses Rogers, is largely the ability to learn.

The black bear is also a highly curious animal—another sign of intelligence. Its explorations of the human environment are not solely motivated by the search for food. Black bears have explored human campsites, sniffing at object after object, grasping each with a forepaw, holding it, turning it, and finally chewing it, apparently more to determine its texture than its caloric content. All while food lay available nearby.

Aesthetic Affiliation

This talk of intelligence leads us onto vulnerable ground. Given the intelligence and social communication of black bears, the individuality of their behavioral profiles, and a recent evolution similar if not convergent to ours—might we suspect that they are aware of their own lives? One wonders if the individual bear feels anything beyond sensory perception, in some emotional sense. Is it even possible that the bear (in her own way, of course), enjoys her life?

I can already hear the denials by detractors, that hardhearted breed of biophysical theorists who base their considerations only on what can be digitized, subjected to multivariate analysis, comprehended and approved by computer. And others, too, who are repulsed by the suggestion (in their interpretation) that bears are humanlike, thus removing the specialness of being human. Lowering our rank or raising the bear's—both are threatening prospects, disturbing, inconceivable. Anthropomorphic at least.

Not so, writes Donald R. Griffin in his *Question of Animal Awareness*. Many animals use language systems. Thought processes, though not necessarily the conscious intent to communicate, are believed to be closely linked to the use of language. This implies, according to Griffin, a "qualitative evolutionary continuity (though not identity) of mental experiences among multicellular animals." By accepting—with caution—the possibility that animals have mental experiences, we may promote our own understanding of the animal. To dismiss the idea as anthropomorphic is to imply that, if aware,

Black bears depend upon newly emerging vegetation, colonial insect larvae, berries, nuts, and acorns in season. Other foods may supplement these mainstays, but if the mainstays are scarce, malnutrition and failed reproduction may occur. The black bear's long sticky tongue helps it obtain large quantities of insect larvae from small cavities in trees and logs.

The three-year-old initiates play. Both bears' ears are spread in the play position. A stiff poke from his large friend knocks the three-year-old down. His ears go back to a defensive position. The large bear still wants to play and has his ears in the spread position. The smaller bear left for awhile. Play is characterized by a lack of vocalizations and by spread ears. It can include restrained biting.

animals would have the same kind of experience as man. This refutation, based on the assumption that human awareness is the only kind of awareness, is what is anthropocentric and thus refutes itself.

"Bears are made of the same dust as we," wrote John Muir, "and breathe the same winds and drink of the same waters. A bear's days are warmed by the same sun, his dwellings are overdomed by the same blue sky, and his life turns and ebbs with the same heart-pulsings as ours." But he also wrote, "They are not companions of men."

What exactly is a black bear? No man can say for certain. Only the bears know, and they aren't telling us. Not yet anyway. If we're planning to learn any more about the bears, we're going to have to sneak back into the woods with them and the unprejudiced biologists already on their trail. The best we can surmise from our current ponderings is that the animal's present shape and design were formed by the forested landscape and prehistoric snows on this continent which we share. The black bear is a creature derived from the cold woods. The bear of America.

Bears are generally shy creatures and avoid humans. When people come within sight of bears, the animals slip quietly away before they are detected.

Black bears are curious and exceptionally quick to learn. They have a heavier brain, compared to body length, than any land animal except the primates. Cubs learn locations of food and how to get it by following and watching their mothers. Old bears, like some older people, grow white hair on their heads. In the wild, bears may live as long as twenty-five years. The oldest known bear of any species was a captive female grizzly that was euthanized at forty-four years of age. She had her last litter only three years prior to her death.

CHAPTER 5

In the month or two prior to hibernation, many black bears range outside their usual range in search of the best food supplies. In northern forests, this "fall shuffle" actually occurs in August and September. Male bears, particularly, travel widely during this period.

Autumn in bear country—cold returning, geese babbling overhead, Orion back on the prowl. These are rich times for the bears and the biologists who watch them. Back in the forest, the black bears shamble around, working overtime to pack in a maximum load of critical, energy-laden rations. They may range far to find good forage. This is the period of hyperphagia, excessive eating, necessary to lay on enough fat to survive the winter and following spring. The bears' daily locations now specify to biologists the habitat types most critical for survival.

The field offices for the New Hampshire black bear research project are located in a small cabin at the end of the road up the east flank of Cherry Mountain. At precisely four a.m. on November 12, Kathleen Meddleton emerges from headquarters. In the darkness she climbs into her research vehicle, a green, beaten four-wheel-drive Fish and Game Department pickup brought out of retirement for this purpose. She descends Cherry Mountain and turns east for a few miles, then pulls off the road under a starless sky. Station number one. She hangs the radio receiver around her neck, charges the luminous dial of her compass by flashlight, and dismounts. In the bed of the truck she raises the Yagi antenna and faces the mountain. When she hears an electronic pulse in her headset, she has found a bear.

Waving the Yagi back and forth in diminishing arcs, she sounds out the loudest signal— her best guess of the direction of the bear from her current position. Sighting down the antenna she picks a corresponding point on the skyline, takes a compass reading, then detaches herself and climbs back into the cab. On a topographical map she traces the proper line through her current locus and up into bear country.

Kathleen is one of two principle researchers on a project designed to take a closer look at the statewide bear population and the effect of hunting upon it. She and Doug Kane are graduate students at the University of New Hampshire, working out of the wildlife department there and in cooperation with the state Fish and Game Department. This fall Kathleen keeps track of ten instrumented bears by determining the whereabouts of each at least once per day, every day.

The study itself was inspired when New Hampshire Fish and Game Department biologist Eric Orff noticed that the percentage of older females in the hunterkill appeared to be decreasing. Such a decline can be a function of a healthy, rapidly growing bear population in which dispersing males are more numerous and conspicuous targets. But it may also indicate a black bear population dwindling under too heavy hunting pressure, which tends to remove older age classes. Harvest data alone cannot provide the distinction. With hunters' growing interest in black bears as big game, and the public's increasing desire to keep the bears as neighbors (at some distance, however), Orff knew he had the same volatile situation a number of other states and provinces have recently faced. He also had a situation where a habitat and black bear population which had been on the rebound for nearly a century were suddenly, insidiously, being threatened again. This time not by sheep pastures and cornfields but by concrete, macadam, and the low hum of high-voltage transformers. It was time, Orff figured, to get a handle on the black bear population.

By following the collared bears Kathleen will determine to some extent how much country each bear covers during each season and what kinds of habitat they prefer. Biologists have performed similar studies for decades and throughout the continent. Doug examines the mortality of females in reference to their vulnerability to different hunting techniques and seasons. He relies on ear tags and hunter questionnaires. (Doug is a hunter, too. Each fall he sallies homeward to Maine, kills a bear, skins it immediately and carves off all the fat as soon as it hardens, rendering steaks of sweet and distinctive flavor. He finds use for the hide and grease as well as the meat.)

Locating her bear from a second pull-off, Kathleen triangulates its position. This time the lines cross in the high country. She presumes that the young female is feeding in a stand of hardwoods, probably beechnuts.

During the fall shuffle, bears are hyperphagic, eating several times their daily energy requirement, if possible, to fatten for hibernation. This sow and her cubs were followed by researchers from the North Central Forest Research Station during late summer and fall. After food became essentially nonexistent in late September, the bear family spent more than twenty-two hours per day resting. Before bears enter their winter dens, their heart rate may drop to as low as twenty-two beats per minute or lower. During this foodless period, they become lethargic, drifting in and out of sleep.

A food habits study based on scat analysis earlier this year indicates that the local bears feed predominantly on grasses from May through July, and then on fruits in August. No surprises here. The Cherry Mountain bears have been feeding predominantly on hard mast since September. Currently, prime food items here appear to be beechnuts, hazelnuts, and mountain ash berries, and of those, primarily beechnuts, most of which are on the ground. Unlike the fumbling antics one might expect, a black bear forages with considerable finesse—carefully fluffing up the leaf litter under a beech tree with it paw, lowering its nose in close-up olfactory search patterns, plucking and chewing the nuts individually. While the nuts are still arboreal, black bears may climb for them, perch on a limb in the crown, and bend in all reachable nut-bearing branches, thus forming a "bear nest." In November these nests become highly visible when the leaves on the injured branches fail to fall. The smooth bark on the trunks of the beeches will retain the indelible claw tracks.

Kathleen motors on, climbing up out of the meadows and alder sloughs and derelict apple orchards and into the pointy timber, pausing intermittently for electronic surveillance. Most of the study bears' home ranges include a full complement of available topography: high and low country, for a range of food options and cover, and a core area in which the bear spends sixty percent of its time. Core areas comprise about one-third of the entire home range and contain a greater composition of softwoods, for cover, and small timber cuts for feeding. This time of year, however, many of the bears cruise the hills for beech stands outside their core areas.

From the pass, Kathleen surveys her study area in the heart of the White Mountains, most of it under the relative protection of the United States Forest Service, a division of the U.S. Department of Agriculture. The habitat here is big enough to get lost in, and has plenty of woods in which black bears can hide, if and when necessary. At least eighty-six black bears are hiding down there right now, each with a numbered aluminum tag in its ear and one tooth

In 1985, food shortages in northeastern Minnesota and Canada triggered bear movements in excess of a hundred miles and possibly far in excess of that distance. The Lake Superior shoreline funnelled bears into Thunder Bay and Duluth, where the bears ate clover, apples, and garbage; one hundred and sixty were shot around the outskirts of those cities alone.

A black bear can climb any tree large enough to support its weight, which helps the black bear compete for food against grizzly bears, deer, and wild pigs.

missing—a premolar for ageing purposes. Everything appears in proper order, with only a few
exceptions. At the foot of the ridge, for example,
Kathleen observes an invading stand of *Condominium
vulgaris* sprouted and spreading like cancer in the
habitat. One more little malignant lump on the breast
of New Hampshire, engendered as usual by
something industrial in the air.

More stops, further biotelemetric interro-
gations. A young male lingers high on Mt. Clay,
having traveled seventeen straight-line miles in just
over twenty-four hours to arrive there yesterday. An
impressive but not unusual feat for a black bear. Late
summer and autumn travels outside regular home
ranges are typical, particularly in years of food
shortage and among mature males. These journeys
may see a black bear range up to one hundred and
twenty-five miles from its home range, only to return,
usually before denning. Gary Alt labelled this
phenomenon the "fall shuffle"; Kathleen uses the
term "sally." The bears travel straightaway, cross-
country, to a concentrated food source—a dump or a
productive stand of oaks—to spend a week or two
feeding there. While they appear to break the pattern
of strict caloric gain and critical energy conservation
of the bear's autumn schedule, these sallies likely
function to verify the presence of emergency food
concentrations for use in a year when really
necessary. Young males one-and-one-half to three-
and-one-half years old combine this behavior with
dispersal out of their mother's territory. The fall
shuffle may coincide with hunting seasons. During
years of lowest or widely scattered mast production,
bears travel most, appear more numerous, cross roads
more frequently (or die in the effort), and fall to the
guns of hunters in greater numbers.

Prior to 1950, accounts of black bear
"migrations" abounded from Crow Wing, Minnesota, to Pine Creek, Pennsylvania, and down to the
Mississippi delta country. These so-called migrations
were characterized by large numbers of bears
following hard-beaten trails away from their usual
range and along rivers to common fording areas, and

they sometimes occurred simultaneously with
emigrations of gray squirrels and wild turkeys. Mast
failures always preceded the migrations; many factors
including higher bear population densities, due to the
availability of more and better habitat and therefore
greater food supply during average and good years,
may have made these autumn travels appear as
migrations. The last of them on record include a black
bear "exodus" from California bear ranges in the fall of
1961, and a mass movement of bears southward off the
Canadian Shield and across northern Minnesota,
toward better soils and mast production, in the fall of
1985. Both occurred during years of food crop failure.

How a black bear finds its way so far and
back again remains a mystery despite recent
investigations into their navigational abilities.
Nuisance bears have been regularly translocated
miles from any familiar range. Some have spent a
week or two in the new country, then disappeared
from it, usually to head in a general homeward
direction. Experienced bears are more likely to
succeed in homing. When translocated they may
circle a few times, sit down, sniff the air, and then take
off toward home at a rate of up to four to five miles
per day, regardless of variable winds, unfamiliar
landscape, and water crossings of several miles. Bears
have returned through strange country from release
points as far as one hundred and forty-two miles from
their home ranges. One sow traveled ninety-eight
miles toward home from over one hundred and sixty-
eight miles away before being shot for suburban
trespass.

A bear that wants to get somewhere specific
within its familiar home range can do so,
and in a straight line. The black bear learns
quickly and remembers well, and what it passes
during dispersal or on sallies it retains on an internal
map.

In their navigations, animal behaviorists
speculate, black bears may plot their own locations
using orientation of magnetic fields, odors on the
wind, or the shape of a hill. The bears obviously
operate more than one guidance system, and some-

When bears travel widely, especially in fall, they sometimes stumble into areas of human habitation. Such animals are often killed as "nuisance" bears.

times may use a combination of cues to find a distant hazelnut stand or to return, at a slow but steady plod, feeding as always along the way, to the sweet security of their home range.

Black bears nearly always come home from their autumn sallies to den. Locations of these den sites are precious to biologists who wish to study hibernation or merely take advantage of a sow's winter sleep to count her cubs. But timing of the onset of denning is valuable knowledge too.

The radio collars in Kathleen's study are equipped with a motion sensor; when a bear lies still for four hours the signal switches to "fast mode" and the audible pulse rate doubles. The first fast mode was signaled in late October from bear number 035, a twenty-two-year-old female who bore no cubs last year. Pregnant sows usually den earliest in populations across Canada and the U.S., followed in order by sows with cubs, barren females and sub-adults, and, finally, adult males. The date of onset of this general sequence varies with geographic location and, from year to year, with food supply. Bears in moderate shape that fail to find food may den early, but hungry bears which find hard mast may feed late into December. Kathleen has a wager, therefore, that 035 is pregnant. A younger female, the mother of three nine-month-old cubs, has been slipping in and out of fast mode too. All bears vacillate between modes—a progressive lethargy—for a week or two prior to holing up for good.

Near the end of her circuit now, Kathleen is standing in the truck bed, incessantly waggling her antenna around in November's evening light. She sways left, right, left, right, arm extended and offering her chrome-plated double-cross-shaped antenna up to an image in the distant woods. Left, right, left, in ever diminishing arcs, her entire body from ankles upward oscillates back and forth in slow, deliberate, trance-like fashion, eyes focused along the skyline, divining the bear.

And she is inwardly celebrating. Somewhere back up there on the flank of Cherry Mountain old lady 035 has slipped into her magical and perfect winter sleep.

Well-fattened bears may cease feeding and retire to dens as early as September, but bears that are less fat may continue to search for food for another one to three months before hibernating.

Although black bears prefer to cover long distances on foot, they are capable swimmers and have often been observed crossing mile-wide waters. When natural foods are scarce, bears travel farther than usual, are seen more often, and are erroneously assumed to be more numerous.

CHAPTER 6

"A bear is wiser than a man because a man does not know how to live all winter without eating anything."
— Abenaki saying

"In an evolutionary sense, hibernation in the bear represents perhaps the most refined response to starvation of any mammal."
— Ralph Nelson, M.D., Ph.D.

The black bear overwinters at home, sparing itself a costly and extravagant migration southward. Any animal which prefers to cozy up alone for the winter—and which voluntarily conserves energy during a period of fuel shortage by turning down the heat and reducing travel—deserves our respect. Point of contention: There are students of the issue who argue that the black bear is not a true hibernator. The black bear, they point out correctly—like the grizzly of the West and the polar bear of Canada—lowers its body temperature only a few degrees and does not fall into the near-freezing comatose state of what they call the "true" hibernators (woodchucks, bats, small rodents, and shrews). They suggest different terminology to define the bears' winter sleep. Call it dormancy, they say, or heavy sleep. Not scientific enough? How about carnivorean lethargy? Seasonal ursine torpor?

Not so fast, say other experts on bear hibernation. These scientists point out that hibernation is generally defined as "an adaptation to periods of food shortage and low environmental temperature," or more specifically as "the specialized seasonal reduction of metabolism concurrent with the environmental pressures of food unavailability and low temperature." Nothing there that a black bear doesn't do. To certify and close the case, however, I consulted my Random House dictionary, which defines hibernation from a different angle, to wit: "to spend the winter in close quarters in a dormant condition, as certain animals." Dormant: "lying asleep or as if asleep; inactive. . . ."

"Black bears may not be hibernators," says Dr. Ralph Nelson of the University of Illinois, but they're "still metabolic marvels." And it remains obvious to other biochemical researchers including Dr. Edward Folk at the University of Iowa that black bears are better at it than the true (sic) hibernators. The woodchuck, the hoary bat, the chipmunk and others may cut their metabolic rates by ninety percent or more and nearly freeze, and reduce heart rate and breathing to almost imperceptible levels while maintaining some level of brain and cardiac function at temperatures which would be lethal to most mammals, but they must arouse themselves periodically. Every few days during hibernation, something triggers within each of them a warm-up process fueled by the metabolism of brown fat. The critter awakens, warms up, shambles off to relieve itself, feeds at its food cache, finds a drink, and in the process restores chemical balances, immune systems, and DNA production, repairs bone cells and nervous tissue, and exercises muscles to avoid atrophy. Without frequent arousal, these hibernators would die of uremic poisoning or ketonemia or wake up with weakened muscles, decalcified bones, degenerated nervous systems, and low immunities.

Bears, however, may curl up for six months or more each year without changing position and without need—during the entire period—to defecate, urinate, eat, or drink. The bear's body chemistry remains healthy without threat of ketosis, uremic poisoning, or dehydration, and with no recognizable muscle atrophy, bone degeneration, or nerve cell disrepair. Upon awakening, the bear may be lighter by twenty or twenty-five percent (up to forty percent lighter for a post-partum sow), but the loss is entirely fat. Lean body mass, including the protein component, has not decreased.

Nelson and Folk also point out that bears are the only animals that carry out gestation and parturition during periods of anorexia. The only animals, in other words, which are pregnant and give birth during starvation. Through a delicate and complex scheme, bears alone have overlapped their reproductive cycle and their adaptation to winter starvation. This scheme allows the starving, sleeping

Hibernation is an adaptation to survive winter food scarcity rather than to escape the cold. Open dens are nearly as cold as the outside air. Bottom: Disapproving of being photographed in her den, this female blew, slapped and threw bedding into the air—her way of saying she is not accepting visitors—when Dr. Lynn Rogers crawled in with his camera.

animal to successfully bear young in the dead of winter and then nurse them through what some call an "external pregnancy." Black bears give birth to such relatively undeveloped young because the mother can more efficiently provide energy to the young through milk than through the placenta, given the constraints of hibernation physiology.

This scheme, complicated as it may appear, relies primarily upon the warm hibernating temperature of bears. The bear mother, whose temperature hovers just a few degrees below the normal summer body temperature of about one hundred degrees, retains brain function—a function of body temperature—and radiates heat for the cubs cuddled next to her uninsulated belly. Even males and barren females maintain temperatures of no lower than eighty-eight degrees during winter sleep.

High body temperature during hibernation is in turn made possible through the bear's bulk (lower surface area to body mass ratio, therefore lower rate of heat loss) and thicker coat. In relation to body weight, the energy cost for a wintering chipmunk to maintain a similar body temperature would become exorbitant, exhaustive, and lethal. The bears, on their own scale, can maintain only slightly lowered thermostats and survive the winter entirely on their own body reserves.

Nothing short of miraculous, one might say. Yet as expert as black bears may be at starvation, the healthiest and most fecund among them live and flourish in the land of greatest providence.

YOU'VE GOT A FRIEND IN PENNSYL-VANIA. That's what it says on all the license plates around here. We're paying a visit to Gary Alt, bear biologist for the Pennsylvania Game Commission. Alt runs the largest bear-tagging program in North America. He keeps ear tags stapled onto some four to six hundred black bears. Here in his Pocono Mountain study area he personally monitors forty radio-collared females—strictly for reproductive data, he says.

Pounding over the Interstate potholes—the chief modern geological characteristic of this state—I admire the countryside around me. Not bad for Pennsylvania. I drive past ridge after long, low ridge, each thickly covered with oak and laurel. Between the uplands lie dark, occluded maple swamps, beaver ponds, and spruce bogs reminiscent of higher latitudes. These features—oak uplands and wet thickets—provide the local bear population with ample autumn food and a place to hide. In their present juxtaposition and integrity, they comprise the best black bear habitat on earth.

But there are a few drawbacks, and we're part of one of them today. Pennsylvania is a land of one hundred thousand miles of paved roads and fifteen million people. As becomes obvious to even the most innocent traveler, there are too many roads and too much traffic. Bears are killed and wasted on these roads. Woodland continues to fall before the coal shovel. Wetlands are drained, dredged for peat moss, then filled in for further development. Behind every ridge now lurks a suspicious, volatile plume. Same old story, so common in its cross-continental folly as to be presumed natural, necessary, inevitable.

"One of the penalties of an ecological education is that one lives in a world of wounds," said Aldo Leopold.

Deep in what's left of Penn's Woods, not far from Lord's Valley, Mountain Home, Paradise Valley, Bear Creek and Promised Land, on a level ridge looking northward over prime bear country, Gary Alt has built his home. I find him here by prearranged appointment this evening in the first week of March, snow falling in the scrub oaks. He appears at his door, grinning as usual, knotting up a green uniform tie. His phone is ringing. We leave immediately for a presentation he is to give tonight. I interview him while we travel.

I begin by asking him exactly what makes this Pennsylvania countryside the best known habitat for black bears. Alt answers in terms of forest cover, high annual mast production, and optimal climate. But the key, he says, is in the structure of the vegetation. Black bears like thick cover, and

Pennsylvania has plenty of that, too.

How do we know Pennsylvania's habitat is the best? Easy, he says. Productivity is highest here. For example, in Montana black bear sows give birth for the first time, on average, at seven or eight years of age, and then bear litters every three years, sometimes less often. In Pennsylvania, forty percent give birth at three years of age and the rest at four. Then they bear litters every other year. These litters are generally larger and grow faster Why? Availability of high-quality foods. Black bears in Pennsylvania are the fattest anywhere.

And what good are obese bears? I inquire. The situation is not comparable to that of humans, Alt explains. An obese bear is a healthy bear. The fat ones survive, and the fatter ones raise more and fatter cubs. They're built to handle the load.

Fine, Gary, I say. But are they any happier, any more contented, let's say, than the bears of Cherry Mountain, New Hampshire? Cabin Creek, Montana? Kawishiwi River, Minnesota? Alt gives me a baleful stare. They sleep better, he says.

Ah, there's the point. This capability to be healthy in obesity is an adaptation to support hibernation. Right, says Alt. One more key twist in the intricate biology of bears, crimped in place under the simple pressure of a winter season.

Hibernation. I mention the disagreement among authors about using the term "hibernation" for the winter sleep of black bears. Does Gary Alt, I wonder, believe his bears hibernate?

Shaking his head, Alt dismisses the argument as one of semantics. We might want to define bear hibernation as a unique case, but we don't need a confusion of terms and definitions here, he tells me.

If bears only eat until they have enough fat for overwintering, then why are Pennsylvania bears so much fatter than others? Because they have enough to eat on a regular basis here, Alt replies. Early season nutrition also sustains skeletal and muscle growth, building a framework capable of foraging better, perhaps, and of carrying more fat.

I attempt to argue with Alt (his uniform elicits my rebellious instincts) about environmental philosophy, politics, and the survival of the natural world as we know it, but the discussion degenerates into agreement. His cynical perspectives, strategically underlain with a determined optimism, sound somehow familiar.

"How long will it be until habitat loss around here begins to threaten the health and population level of your bear population?" I ask. His answer surprises me.

"It isn't food or cover that limits the number of bears in Pennsylvania," he tells me. "It's the human attitudes. We are losing habitat, especially wetland, way too fast, but the land will clearly support many more bears than the people of this state will tolerate."

"Fear?" I ask.

"Fear, nuisance problems, too many misconceptions."

"It's the old problem of overpopulation," I suggest. "Too many people."

"It's the attitude," says Alt. "Bears can live near people. It isn't the bears that lack the ability to adapt; it's the people. Remember that."

I think of what Eric Orff is beginning to see in southern New Hampshire, and I ask Alt if he knows of any other states in which this is the case.

"Some people look at Pennsylvania and say it's an anomaly," he says. "I say, 'Take a good look—this is the future.' "

"Is that a threat?"

"That . . . is an observation."

I ask him what are the most popular public misconceptions about hibernating bears. Probably aggression and the reuse of dens, he says. Aggression, I say, even during hibernation? Yes, he says, the fear of bears is pervasive. Are there any incidents to substantiate this? Alt recounts for me a number of stories about bears, freshly awakened from winter sleep, rushing in their escape inadvertently toward him or a technician. "Nearly all

While one of her cubs rests, a mother and her second cub rake leaves, grass, and clubmoss backward into their den. Although rock dens like this one will last for centuries, they are seldom re-used by the same bears. During hibernation, bears maintain a body temperature above eighty-eight degrees, enabling them to continue mental function and other physiological maintenance. Thus, mothers can respond to non-hibernating cubs' cries and care for them.

of us have been run over by a black bear at one time or another," he says. But no one injured? No one.

As for den reuse, the frequency is very low, according to Alt's findings, which are corroborated by other observations in Arizona, Idaho, Minnesota and the Smoky Mountains. Only five to six percent of known bear dens are re-used during any year, and less than half of these cases involve the same bear. The rarest thing, says Alt, is the reuse of the same den by the same bear on consecutive years.

Female bears in Pennsylvania tend to select more secure dens than males, and are more likely to re-use a den, particularly when pregnant. A daughter is about one-fourth as likely to re-use her natal den as her mother is to re-use it. From the manner in which disturbed bears often move straight to a different den in mid-winter, Alt surmises that most black bears remember the locations of former or potential dens within their home ranges. Multiple den sites and low reuse may offer an adaptive advantage against winter predation of the cubs. And because black bears use a variety of kinds of dens, the availability of den sites appears not to be a limiting factor, except in one study on a small island off the coast of Washington where researchers found fifty percent den reuse. Den sites there may have been limited due to island terrain and recent extensive logging, or the small bear population may have developed a cultural behavior quirk.

What about finding more than one bear in a den? Cohabitation, says Alt, except for a sow and her cubs, is virtually nonexistent. Only one case has been reported: In Ontario, researchers recently found a sow with two cubs sharing her den with a two-year-old male.

I thought of something Kathleen Meddleton had said to me in New Hampshire—that her bears sometimes denned outside their home ranges on the way back from their fall sallies. Reports in the literature often suggest that black bears den within their home ranges. This might be important, I thought, in the clarification of exactly what a black bear's home range is, and in reference to the importance of den selection. I put all this to Alt.

He replies that his bears appear always to den within their home ranges. No exceptions? No. He pauses, then says, "But we have to be very careful in interpreting bear movements. Home ranges are infinitely dynamic." Likely outside the realm of human statistical descriptions? I ask. Likely, he says. We're trying to box in something that doesn't exist in constant shape. Semantics again. Definitions.

As food availability changes, and as bear behavior changes from spring breeding to radical autumn feeding, bear movements change to accommodate the variables. "A home range is really a bear's movements integrated with its social behavior. It's all a matter of logistics." The idea of a home range, then, is another scientific tool to assist us in approximating a bear's movements and habitat use, but not to accurately describe either. When you think of home ranges for bears, Alt says, think plasticity.

After his presentation, we motor back into Alt's home range and straight to his home. It is after midnight, but we stay up, expecting visitors. We are awaiting the arrival of three orphaned cubs from New York.

Each year Alt arranges the adoptions of a dozen or so cubs orphaned when their mothers are road-killed or abandoned when the sows are frightened off by logging or development operations. (Sows rarely return for their cubs when run off during hibernation.) Alt unites his orphans with his radio-collared sows at a success rate of over ninety percent. Lynn Rogers in Minnesota and John Beecham in Idaho have reported similar success, though Rogers notes that in his sub-optimum habitat, females with litters enlarged through adoption to more than three cubs may need supplemental food in order to successfully nurse the brood.

Natural adoption by black bears is extremely rare, but natural instincts make the artificial approach surprisingly easy. Alt found he could place an orphan near the den entrance of a hibernating nursing mother, let it bawl in the cold, and in seconds

Although newborn cubs do not hibernate, adults must in order to ration their fat, which is metabolized over the five to seven months of northern winters. Although the clean odor of a hibernating bear is detectable even by humans, most animals ignore it. Deer and moose browse on top of dens. Wolves investigate primarily the dens of injured bears. During a study of two hundred and six occupied dens in northern Minnesota, nine wolves killed and ate the occupants of one den.

the sow would appear, grunting and sniffing, to carry the cub inside. Sows apparently do not recognize their own cubs by smell during hibernation.

Cubs offered to nursing females after den emergence, however, were usually killed or abandoned, apparently due to olfactory cues. So Alt had to get trickier. He rubbed Vicks Vapo-Rub onto the sow's nose or the orphan's fur or both. Or he confined the orphan with the natural cubs for two hours or more before returning the entire brood to the sow. Through both techniques the orphan acquired family scent from its new siblings before the mother had the opportunity to collect olfactory data on the newcomer. The "Vicks fix," says Alt, is fast and easy.

Alt recounts the time he attempted the technique on a sow who had left her den with five cubs. He had a pair of orphans and thought he'd give her one. (Natural litters of six are not unheard of in Pennsylvania, and besides, says Alt, she was a good mother.) When he treed her and the family that day, however, he counted only three cubs, so he thought, what the hell, we'll give her both orphans. He rubbed them down with Vicks and chased them up the tree. The adoption was processed in the forest canopy in what Alt admits was a rather dense tree crown. He waited nearby to certify success. After several hours the entire family descended—sow and seven cubs. Was Alt surprised? A lot more than the bear, he says.

"Did they all survive?"

"Of course," says Alt, grinning, "This is Pennsylvania."

The Vicks fix works into early June, at which time bottle-fed cubs may begin to imprint on their human captors and reject an adoptive mother. Then what? Raise them with as little human contact as possible and release them in some very remote site. Hope for the best. Some cubs are self-sufficient at five months of age, but Alt recommends release at fifteen to eighteen months.

"How remote a site are you talking about?"

"Somewhere in Idaho."

One a.m.: sound of a car in Alt's driveway. A clatter at the door. In walk Don "Jake" Stunzi, his wife, Lois, and Craig Russell, a veterinarian from Westport, New York. In a cardboard box are three squealing bear cubs. Jake, an electrical contractor from north of the border, works for Alt as a seasonal technician on this project. Like all others involved, he feels privileged, appears devoted, and remains clear of mind and in good humor in the middle of a midwinter night. His first question involves official clearance from the authorities for his interstate cargo. Alt nods.

"Well, have you got a place for these little guys?"

"We've got twenty nursing sows out there sending us signals," says Alt. "Plenty of room."

These orphans could not be placed with sows in New York since there is no current study there with radio-collared sows. No one knows where the potential adoptive mothers have denned. New Jersey would have been the preferred destination, but no one could raise biologist Patricia McConnell over there. She's probably in the field now, too. Too bad, says Jake. The New Jersey population could have used the female. Does Jake regret not placing these cubs with New York mothers? Nah, he says. Many of the subadult males from the Poconos disperse up into the Catskills anyway. And Alt has a good idea of which of his bears are the best mothers, most preferred for adoption. Not just any bear is chosen; they go on a case-by-case basis. And Alt knows his cases, says Jake.

Stunzi has had the cubs for three weeks, ever since they were picked up after their mother was killed by a poacher. He judges their age at seven weeks now, because their eyes just opened a little over a week ago. The same day their eyes peeled open, he says, they developed a corneal response and immediately began to grasp things in their tiny paws.

I peer into the box at three coal-black pot-bellied puppies with human voices and claws sharp as fishhooks. The automatic instinct is to adopt one yourself.

Black bear mothers readily adopt orphaned cubs. This sow is trying to catch a three-month-old cub whose mother abandoned it when their surface den was disturbed by hikers. The cub, taken to its new mother by wildlife officials, was initially fearful of its new mother and tried to flee from her. Eventually, the adoption was successful.

"You measure them?" says Alt.

"We measured everything but the squeal," says Jake. Everything down to the length of hair between their ears, I find out. According to Alt, the hair on their crowns grows at constant rate, regardless of weight or nutrition, and is therefore the most accurate measurement of age of young cubs.

Five of us share the three a.m. feeding responsibilities. The term "external pregnancy" comes to mind; I look around the room. The cubs cling to us—powerfully, it seems to me—and to their bottles of puppy milk replacer, prescribed and supplied by Craig the vet. They'll double their weight in three weeks, says Alt.

Sated, the cubs bunk out in the basement while someone manages to stir up a few ounces of a different formula for us upstairs. Alt's home begins to feel more like a halfway house for orphaned bears and part-time biologists. We wander off to our various rooms.

The next morning (about three hours later) we repeat the mammalian feeding rituals for the bears and then feed ourselves. More people appear—friends, family, technicians—to see the cubs. Alt and Stunzi head to the basement to sort through equipment, notebooks, vials of fresh drugs, new collars, ear tags, old darts, and dart guns. Today is Alt's first day of the year afield to catch up with his instrumented bears.

Like most other radio followers of the black bear, Alt waits until March to visit dens and disturb the new mothers. By now the worst of winter is over and the cubs are seven or eight weeks old. You want to finish before the bears wake up, so Alt will be afield every day for the next three weeks. A busy but not lonely itinerary.

For example, Alt expects thirty people to go out with us today. A light day, he tells me. He'll have an average of fifty people per day accompanying him. He's taken over seventy at one time to a single den. He'll take twenty or thirty state senators, the governor's family, or the entire second shift from the local shoe factory. As far as I can determine, I tell

him, he's the first and the worst of professional bear den trip leaders. This makes him smile.

"You can't believe the impact," he says. "At a public hearing somebody will stand up and make an irate negative comment about bear management here, and before I can reply someone else in the crowd will stand up and defend our work and say, 'How the hell do you know? Have you ever been out with Alt? Well, I have,' and so on. In the political arena, other people can fight your battles better than you can." A similar approach, he says, worked effectively in the southern Appalachians. Some families down there had poached bears for generations. There appeared to be no way to stop them. Then a few researchers enlisted their aid to find and capture bears, pull teeth, attach collars, track movements. "And then the law of the land changed," says Alt, "and the locals were suddenly defending *their* bears."

As usual, the root of unnatural pressures on the natural world is human behavior, formed and informed by human attitudes. But the answers to the problems lie within the attitudes of the perpetrators as well. And the best way to invoke the answers, to change the attitudes, is through involvement. Alt spends a lot of time, extra time, his own time, scheduling his visitors and offering his evening presentations. Shaping, enlightening, redirecting human attitudes is an overtime job, but Alt sees it as facing-down his limiting factor. He's providing for the future good of his countrymen and the bears.

Drugs all premeasured; darts loaded; charges, ear tags, and other presorted trappings packed into the traditional plastic tackle boxes; receiver and batteries checked; folding Yagi antenna in place; and Number One orphan tattooed, fed and carefully packed in Stunzi's coat; we head out.

At the Whistlestop Store, rendezvous point for today's entourage, we find only four people. "I don't know if we can work a bear today," Alt says, winking at me. "We don't have a quorum." But a dozen miles later, when Alt stops our lead truck to

unfold the Yagi, I notice that our tour has mysteriously grown to seven vehicles and at least sixteen people. That, says Alt, is a quorum. We proceed into Penn's Woods—seventeen human attitudes in search of the innocent bear.

Something mystifies the human comprehension about the presence of an animal not unlike ourselves, lying there in the ground under the winter snow—appearing near lifeless yet still alive and most capable of full resurrection come springtime. Alt told me about one of his study bears which once denned near the vacation home of a family from New York. The entrance to the den faced directly into their dining room window from twenty-two feet away. When Alt mentioned this to the owners, they erected a fence between the two seasonal establishments. Under similar circum-stances, others have moved away.

Perhaps because there is no telltale odor from urine or feces, hibernating bears are rarely sniffed out. Dogs have walked right past bears denned in highway culverts in New Jersey; Alt has seen evidence of deer browsing immediately above a hibernaculum. He once found a bear denning under a cabin in the woods, within three feet of the bunk in which the hunter in residence took his own rest. (Still, Lynn Rogers identifies occupied winter dens versus vacant ones by what he describes as a distinctive "fresh" bear odor. He reports, too, that denned bears that are injured or wounded may give off odors, from infected flesh, for example, and that timber wolves in the Superior National Forest inspect bear dens in winter to detect such vulnerable bears. In one instance he knows of, a wolf pack extracted a hibernating sow and her two cubs from their den, killing and eating all three. Little evidence was left to determine if the sow had suffered a wound previous to hibernating that winter.)

In Pennsylvania, Alt sees about half of the bears denning on the ground and not in it. Particularly the males, he says, which virtually never use a rock cavity or excavation. Sows, especially pregnant ones, are more likely to be in the earth or under dense brush piles. Fewer than one-third of his bears actually excavate under trees or enlarge old fox dens. Some find cover under tree roots or in thickets of young pine. There's no shortage of den sites here, he says, because a bear will den just about anywhere.

In the southern Appalachians, black bears (pregnant sows in particular) prefer to climb up into hollow trees. Tree dens offer greater protection then ground dens from human disturbance and spring floods, and greater insulation against winter temperatures at those latitudes. Bears still use an occasional tree den in Maine, however, and probably used a lot more of them throughout northern hardwood and mixed forests when large trees were more numerous. In colder climates, where radiant heat from the earth becomes more of a consideration, black bears select ground dens more frequently. Sows emerging with cubs like to be near a big rough-barked pine for escape insurance.

Entrances to excavated dens are typically only as large as necessary to allow the occupant to enter. In-earth dens average about nineteen cubic feet in volume; forty-five of them would fit into a nine-by-twelve bedroom.

Black bears line most dens with grasses, leaves, club mosses, fir boughs, cedar bark, even fragrant Labrador tea (where available), all of it gathered from within fifty feet of the site. The process appears instinctive, since orphaned cubs have exhibited the behavior alone in their first autumn. It is also an imprecise one, accomplished in what Lynn Rogers once called a "languid and listless" fashion by individuals on their downward glide into winter sleep. Whatever is close and looks appropriate is used. In Minnesota, Greg Wilker once hung an activated radio collar near the den of a bear he'd been following that fall. In March he followed the signal back to the den in order to attach the collar to the sleeping bear, but at the site he found no collar. The cooperative bear had carried it into her nest. (This was not the first time a black bear had made off with a human possession to line its nest. In northwestern Minnesota in the late 1890s a

Medical researchers are trying to learn how black bears avoid problems of bone degeneration, muscle atrophy, waste accumulation, and physiological imbalance while hibernating for up to seven months without activity, food, and water, and without urinating or defecating. Hibernating bears can maintain a near-normal core body temperature while burning calories at only half their usual rate because they reduce blood flow to their extremities, grow extremely insulative fur, and remain inactive.

man named Johnson laid down his buffalo robe to tend his horses. When he returned, it was gone. He followed a trail in the snow and found his coat under a black bear in a hole in the ground.)

Of how and where we might expect to find bear dens, little more can be said. Preference of aspect appears variable, dubious at best. In most professional observations, bears tend to select well-drained areas away from human traffic, but many exceptions persist. Today we are locating one of them by radio.

I hold the Yagi out the window while Alt drives the dead-end road along a small tributary. She's not far from the road, he suspects. We make three passes to zero in, then Alt halts the motorcade. He and Jake jog out into the snowy woods and return in a few minutes. The sow is exactly where they left her in October. Gear is apportioned out, and we enter the woods.

We now have not one but two video photographers with us. Everyone's filming documentaries these days. In all my visits this winter, I've been to only one bear den without the encumbrance of someone lugging all that ridiculous gear and then trying to direct operations. But the two videocams today are official. One, belonging to a local TV station, is carried by a short, broad-shouldered young man with too little clothing on and too many bear stories (all climaxing as usual in great horror—but no contact). The other is shouldered by a freelancer for a TV station in New York near where the cubs were found; he wears zippered shoes and doubleknit trousers. Both request at the outset to be first on the scene and closest to the site. Alt allows this, then turns to the rest of us as Jake and the directors move in. "We always let these guys go in first," he explains thoughtfully. "They're pretty slow with all that gear, so we'll be able to get out if we have to."

Sly laughter from the gallery. Alt is known for his ability to handle a crowd.

We pick our way for several minutes through the brushy woods, and then we stop. At the edge of a maple swamp one hundred and fifty yards from the road, a hundred yards from the railroad tracks beyond, we find the innocent bear. Ninety miles due north and a half million years this side of the oldest known black bear, whose bones were discovered in the cave in Port Kennedy on the Schuylkill River, lies the living carcass of a contemporary *Ursus americanus*, deep in her magical sleep by a tributary of Roaring Brook. The quintessential black bear, I'm thinking, surprised again at the very spectacle I expected to see. The mind reaches for descriptive words.

"Her name is Lucky," says Alt.

Lucky is a pure black mass against a landscape white with several inches of snow. The ground around her is a thicket of marsh weeds and berry canes about waist high, or at eye level for an adult bear—characteristic of most of the den sites I've seen this winter. Her luxuriant fur shines in the Pennsylvania sunlight. She lies face down, her forehead pressed against the root mass of a drowned and fallen red maple. Her butt is curled forward on the ground, haunches folded, and her forelegs are cradled beneath her abdomen. Thus positioned, she exposes the denser fur of the back, neck, and sides—currently thickened to twice its summer insulation—to the open air. She folds her less-insulated muzzle, legs, and underside within. From the central interior of this mass we hear the tremulant hum of nursing cubs.

Even so insulated, Lucky is starkly visible to us today not simply because she has nested above ground, but also because she continues to practice her homeothermic prerogative—she is still warm. She has melted off her snow cover. In her sleep, even without cubs, she continues to burn up to 4,000 kilocalories per day—a rate of energy expenditure approximating half her summer metabolic rate, or that of a white-tailed deer foraging all day. Lucky is both heat factory and insulated thermal mass. In contrast to the subfreezing air, the temperature on the outer edge of a three-inch thick coat overlaying another three inches of insulating fat remains above freezing (until the ambient temperature drops below

Black bears investigate potential dens all summer long but can hibernate only between April and September. Food shortage in summer causes starvation. Bears gradually enter hibernation over a period of weeks in fall and regain activity over a few weeks in spring, a period called "walking hibernation." This family rested for two weeks after food became scarce and then entered a den on October 11.

eight degrees Fahrenheit, at which time the snow would lay on her). If she were not warm, of course, neither would be her cubs, and they are not hibernating. Lucky manages all this without the necessity for exercise, feeding, drinking, urinating or defecating at any time during hibernation.

The functional key to hibernation is fat. Lucky burns only fat during hibernation, depending on the large store of it accumulated through her autumn foraging. Since she eats nothing, she need not defecate, though natural sloughing of the intestinal lining will fill her bowels by spring emergence. (Some bears have been observed to defecate during the winter, particularly when disturbed.) Fat catabolism produces more energy per gram of fuel than the burning of either protein or carbohydrate. It also produces more water as a by-product, and this metabolic water fills all of the bear's winter hydration needs.

Still, water requirements remain low during hibernation because urine production is greatly reduced. Urine is necessary to pass the nitrogenous waste product of protein metabolism, urea, from the mammalian body. But because black bears burn almost entirely fat during hibernation, they produce little urea, and therefore form little urine. What urine is produced by the kidney—about a third the summer production—is reabsorbed through the bladder wall, preventing bladder distention and the need for arousal and that little walk.

While little or no protein is metabolized now for energy and heat production, protein "turnover" (the normal process of breaking down and renewing protein structures in the mammalian body) actually accelerates, producing some urea. The hibernating black bear recycles this waste along at least two pathways, both complex and not entirely understood. Along one pathway, the urea in the blood is broken down into carbon dioxide, water, and ammonia. The ammonia then combines with glycerol (another by-product of the burning of fat) to form new amino acids, and in turn new proteins for body repair. The second pathway, less certain at this time, also recycles

the nitrogen from urea into new protein.

Through the winter, the net result of these two "nitrogen shuttle" pathways is, in the average bear, the incorporation of three grams of urea nitrogen into twenty-one grams of protein—about the amount of protein required to construct one newborn cub. The enhanced protein turnover rate provides a nitrogen source from urea, radiates a little extra heat, may help keep nerves and muscles from atrophying, and may even allow Lucky to synthesize her own essential amino acids.

The net effect of winter starvation on the black bear, then, is the loss of only fat (through the production of heat, water, and glycerin for a protein shuttle) and no loss of lean body mass. For healthy bears at least. A bear that runs low on fat during hibernation and begins to metabolize protein for heat will poison the pathways, become uremic, be forced to urinate, and likely die in the den. Lynn Rogers has visited the den of a thin bear and recognized the failure of its hibernation mechanism by the rare odor of ammonia there.

Dr. Nelson has also postulated that since fat metabolism in hibernation fails to produce ketosis in bears, another pathway may exist which recycles fatty acids (the components of fats which produce ketone bodies) by combining them with glycerol in the blood to rebuild triglycerides (fat deposits). An excess of ketone bodies in the blood is a symptom of diabetes mellitus in humans. A very similar condition is believed to trigger the periodic arousal of the "true" hibernators.

During all of this, the bear further conserves energy by reducing peripheral blood flow. While the heart rate is generally lowered to eight to ten beats per minute from forty to fifty, it appears to rise about once each day, possibly to assist in body and biochemical system maintenance. A specific acid is secreted to dissolve cholesterol gallstones formed by the metabolism of fat. Bears may have a unique and secret calcium and phosphorus mechanism too, which maintains healthy bones during their winter sleep.

Perfect as the strategy and techniques may

Sometimes mothers must move cubs when their dens become flooded. This mother was exceedingly careful to grasp the cub gently, using her paw to place the cub far in her mouth behind her canine teeth.

be, there remains one shortcoming, one major qualification. The black bear, like the grizzly, can only hibernate in winter. Even under laboratory conditions of artificially reduced temperatures, day length, and under a starvation regime, the hibernation mechanism fails to fire up in the summertime. Wild bears starving in July cannot hole up and go to sleep to conserve their energy. Hibernation is strictly a winter strategy.

Through their research, Nelson and many field biologists have garnered a working insight into the black bear's annual physiological cycle. For purposes of our discussion here, we begin in July.

During normal summer activity, bears probably break even, on average, in the balance between energy input and expenditure. Captive animals consume between 5,000 and 8,000 kilocalories per day at this time of year.

In the fall, which may begin as early as July for a North Country bear, feeding accelerates, and on decent ranges the food items include more concentrated energy. During the stage of hyperphagia (literally, "overeating"), our great American bear may feed twenty or more hours per day, consuming 15,000 to 20,000 kilocalories. Fat lays on by the pound.

What follows may be called walking hibernation. Something triggers the onset of the physiological hibernation mechanism, a complex undertaking, as we have seen, which required two or three weeks to warm up. Appetite and thirst begin to abate. Fat stores come into exclusive metabolic use; urea production and urea content in the blood decline. Blood content of creatine, a nitrogen-containing compound used in the energy metabolic pathway, increases. Blood flow to the limbs and other peripheral areas gradually decreases. Biochemical hibernation is underway. Our bear slows down on its feet, seeks a den site, drags together a winter nest.

By the time the ratio of urea to creatine in the blood has decreased from summer levels of twenty or more down to ten, our bear is officially in hibernation, and the involved mechanisms are

running fully at a cost of from 1,000 to 4,000 kilocalories per day.

The duration of hibernation depends largely on the duration of winter foodless conditions. Florida bears den for about two months; North Carolina bears den for three. Denning periods in the South may not even overlap, some bears—males especially—may remain active through the cool season, or drop into winter sleep for two weeks at a time. Black bears den up for four to five months in Pennsylvania, New York, and Arizona, five to seven months in New Hampshire, Maine, and Minnesota, and so on into Canada. In the coldest outback of the Yukon Territories, black bear hibernation may last seven months or more.

Our bear emerges from the den much as it went in—in a state of walking hibernation, active and alert, but biochemically stiff. The readjustment to summer levels may take from two to four weeks, during which time the bear will eat and drink little and pass little urine. A black bear from the suburbs of Dawson City, Yukon Territory, which spends seven months in its hole, therefore, spends eight or nine months per year, or up to seventy-five percent of its life, at some level of biochemical hibernation.

Denning emergence appears to be regulated in general by time of year and proximately by snowfall, decreasing atmospheric pressure (late autumn), and temperature changes. Food availability may play a variable role. But what actually triggers hibernation, the biochemical mechanism? Good question, and difficult to answer.

Dr. Folk and other investigators have been searching for their "hibernation induction trigger" for years and have turned up evidence of one in the blood chemistry of woodchucks and ground squirrels. When injected into other mammals—even non-hibernators—the substance rearranges hormone levels and induces a reaction similar to winter sleep. No similar agent has surfaced in the blood chemistry of black bears.

Nelson and company, however, have tracked a reduced level of thyroid gland function in

Mothers with cubs are usually the last to emerge, sometimes remaining in dens until May. Young bears grow quickly in their first few weeks of life, subsisting on their mother's milk, which is nearly one-third fat. Cow and human milk are only three to five percent fat.

hibernating bears. The thyroid exerts a major control over metabolic rate and is controlled in part by secretions from the pituitary, another gland of the mammalian endocrine (hormonal) system. The pituitary's effect on the thyroid is modulated, in turn, by a third gland, the hypothalamus, which also affects kidney and bladder function. Hypothalamus function—and therefore kidney, bladder, and metabolic function—is affected by changes in food intake. Nelson reports that during winter starvation the black bear's hypothalamus causes the reduction in thyroid stimulation of metabolism. Herein may lie a portion of the complex circuitry that triggers and controls the hibernation mechanism.

Interestingly, the polar bear can hibernate anytime. In terms of the stages noted above, the polar bear exists in a nearly constant state of walking hibernation, even while active. It hibernates for only seven or eight weeks in winter, to give birth, but may den up in summer—in bona fide biochemical hibernation—even when ambient temperatures are warmest.

Why the difference? The answer, like the questions which would follow it, promises to be complex, but one factor stands out in light of our discussion here: fat.

The black bear changes its diet by season, eats little fat, and hibernates only while living on its own fat stores. The polar bear eats almost exclusively fat, in the form of blubber, and can hibernate anytime.

Is it possible, then, that a fat-based metabolism not only allows bears to hibernate by reducing urea production to recyclable levels, but also comprises the triggering mechanism? Perhaps the black bear fails to hibernate in July because the hypothalamus (or some other screening gauge) notices that fat reserves aren't there in proper abundance. Dr. Nelson notes that, in at least some black bears, biochemical hibernation begins the moment the last calorie of stored fat necessary for overwintering is laid on. Regardless, he says, of food availability at the time. Alt and others have noticed that males, particularly subadults, often stay out foraging later than other bears; subadult males would be expected to range farthest and across strange habitat, therefore foraging less efficiently and accumulating fat more slowly. During autumns of food shortage, bears near their caloric quotas may fall into the energy conservation scheme of hibernation while those whose fat stores are too far from sufficient remain at large to forage longer. If true, this would also help explain the disparity among observations of early and late denning during years of low food abundance. The picture of course is complicated further by other variables such as fitness of individual bears, kinds of and dispersion of foods, and weather conditions.

Regardless of the certainty of our final speculation here, fat itself is of major and primary importance to the hibernating black bear. It insulates the animal, supplies the most efficient production of heat and metabolic water while allowing metabolic maintenance with little urea production and, therefore, no need to get up and urinate. The mere presence of fat may allow or trigger biochemical hibernation. Even reproduction depends upon the presence of fat; the blastula will not implant onto the uterine wall unless enough fat is present in the body. One tends to agree with Alt that a fat bear is a healthy bear. Or, to paraphrase Darwin: Only the fat survive.

There we go again, suffering the complex headaches of deep scientific theory when all we're really trying to do is understand a fellow species a little better. What good is all this biochemical research? Who cares whether we know the precise techniques by which the bear survives winter in a hole in the ground and what prods her awake in April?

The pure technology itself is of interest to some, as usual. But above all, as always, by scrutinizing the behavior and internal operations of our fellow species we learn something more about ourselves. It never fails. A number of the results summarized above have been compared to and in some cases applied to the human medical condition.

Gallstones, for example, have been dissolved

Mothers respond to the cries of their cubs to clean them, warm them, nurse them, and to avoid lying on them. Mothers also eat the cubs' feces for the first several weeks after they are born.

out of human gall bladders *in vivo* through application of the acid produced automatically by bears for the same function. Diet control mimicking the hibernating bear already reduces the frequency of need for dialysis among humans with kidney disease. Atherosclerosis, muscle cramps, bone calcium loss, renal disease, lack of blood circulation in sedentary patients, and anorexia nervosa may all be treated in humans one day using the techniques and formulas developed by bears for similar situations during winter sleep. Skin regeneration over severe burns may be accelerated if human protein production could be accelerated as protein turnover is in wintering bears. The bears' ability to avoid ketosis while on fat fuel efficiency, absence of toxic wastes, budget balancing, and productivity all have potential applications in human medicine. There are even those who would apply the merits of bear hibernation toward suspended animation of humans, as would be required in long-term space travel.

So much for the explanation and application of miracles. "The miracle is nowhere but circulating in the veins of man," said Seferis. "We have a lot to learn," says Alt.

What may appear to some of us to be a miracle, and to others an accidental aberration in biochemical physiology, is neither new or different. Diving marine mammals reduce peripheral blood flow and heart rate to conserve energy. Mammals of four other orders drop their metabolic rates to conserve energy and their own lives through the cold and foodless winter. With no water available, domestic dogs reabsorb urine back into their bodies through the bladder wall. After five or six weeks of starvation, obese humans increase utilization of body fat, cut back catabolism of lean body mass, and reduce urea production. (Quite similar to ursine hibernation, these reactions further indicate that the key process of hibernation is a response to food shortage and not cold.) Humans suffering from anorexia nervosa exhibit a hypothalamic response to absence of dietary intake and a decrease in metabolic rate, heart rate, and body temperature.

The hibernating bear performs no new miracles, just the same old ones. Bears have simply fine-tuned the normal mammalian responses to thirst and starvation—and taken them to extremes.

The real miracle by the Roaring Brook swamp today is that all of this theory and biochemistry and endocrinal communication and energy conservation—and motherhood as well—is occurring right here under the cover of a living bear hide, out under the winter sky. In this dark ball of mammalian tissue we have at once proof for the doubting mind, and an incredible display of life in its potential state. Dead but alive . . . that "no place between" again.

Alt and Stunzi have seen it before. They are working biologists, after all. Familiar with miracles. The two gunmen fall out into a crossfire. If she runs, a second shot will ensure her immobilization and survival of the family. Alt fires first, planting a red-flagged dart into her left shoulder. No immediate reaction. Ten seconds later she raises her heavy head, looks directly at us, returns to her original position. We can hear at least two cubs squalling now. Minutes pass. Human attitudes record the scene. Video cameras hum. Alt fears the dart may have failed to inject. A second shot is possible, due to the bear's wide tolerance to the drug Alt uses. This dart drives home and, active instantly, the sow runs off, leaving four little cubs in a writhing pile at the center of the patch of bare ground which is her nest.

While the cubs are not in hibernation, no excrement is obvious here. Lucky not only keeps them warm and guides their little muzzles to her nipples in her subconscious caretaking, she also laps up their defecations and, in the process, stimulates them to urinate and catches the liquid they lose. The milk she feeds them is liquified entirely with metabolic water from her body; she conserves and recycles this water by retrieving it with their feces and urine. The concept of "external pregnancy" revivified.

Later, Alt would tell me that he believes pregnant sows are the deepest hibernators, but become the lightest sleepers once the cubs are born.

In spring, prior to vacating the hibernaculum for good, mothers sometimes briefly leave the cubs sleeping in the den to go feed on willow catkins and to find water.

This may be a function of a slight increase in body temperature associated with muscular movement for cub care. Levels of brain and muscle activity are functions of body temperature. True hibernators are dead, limp, asleep; bears, as we see today, can be awakened. "In any event," says Alt, "we don't count heartbeats by ear or take rectal temperatures without drugging our bears, like Rogers does in Minnesota. We just don't see that degree of lethargy."

Alt hastily delivers commands to us all. Only the video people avoid responsibility. The cubs are rescued and delivered to the warm sanctity of individual parkas, while six of us grab a military stretcher and follow the bear. Alt's only concern is that we don't let her get into any water as the drug takes effect. She could drown. We follow her tracks into a stand of hemlock where Alt is already watching her go down safely. He certifies her stupor, and we take turns, four at a time, lugging two hundred and forty-four pounds of eight-year-old gelatinous ursine protoplasm back to the den site.

By the time the ambulance crew returns, Jake has measured the cubs (length, neck, chest) and weighed them. The three males are all within a few ounces of four pounds; the female weighs three. Our orphan weighs in at three and a half. None appears in danger of starving. Born at about twelve ounces, they'll emerge in April at ten pounds.

Alt tells us these cubs were born on January 14th, plus or minus one day. He knows when to check for birth among his pregnant collared sows because virtually all of the cubs here are born between January 1 and 27, with a strong peak in the middle of that period. Fairly precise timing for an animal which may be in estrus from May into September. Obviously, the delayed implantation of the developing blastulas in all these sows in the fall must be synchronized, but how? Here again, no one knows. "It must be photoperiod," says Alt. "Everything else is too variable."

Lucky has lost an ear tag, which Alt replaces. He exchanges her old collar for a new one (fresh batteries) and shows us a huge scar across her abdomen. Apparently she was twisted up in a snare or wire fence at one time, he explains. Lost one nipple, but survived, so she's Lucky. She's lazy, too, says someone in the crowd, considering her barren nest. Alt allows he's seen better nests, but notes that if Lucky had excavated something here on this flat, she'd be up to her long hairs in snowmelt by now.

Alt and Stunzi give Lucky a quick check-up, and Alt extracts a sample of her milk, a semiliquid of twenty-five to thirty-three percent fat content (cow and human milks contain about three percent fat), and five kilocalories of energy per gram. Of bear species checked, the black bear produces the richest milk, lowest in carbohydrates, highest in casein, ash, calcium and phosphorous. Alt will send this sample to the National Zoo so biologists there can copy its formula for use with panda cubs.

We carry Lucky back to her frugal nest, where Alt carefully positions her exactly as we found her, and inserts all five cubs, one for each nipple. The cubs are suckling as we leave. Jake will return this evening to make certain Lucky hasn't moved after the drugs wear off. We tromp back out to the cars. Alt has to return twice, finally with a vengeance, to retrieve the Spielbergs.

In the end I leave them all behind in the bright Pennsylvania sunshine, the two remaining orphans drinking their formula, Alt preparing for another distant speaking engagement tonight, the veterinarian pondering analytically the cubs' development. "Their ear canals should be opening now," he says by way of a farewell. "If only I had more time with them." And happy Jake, laying plans for tomorrow's adoptions. I wish them all, cubs in particular, good luck.

An hour south of the Pocono Mountains, I drive out of snow cover.

Cubs newly emerged from the den are not adept climbers, but they learn quickly.

When grass sprouts emerge, bears shed the last of their winter lethargy and begin the annual race to consume as much energy-rich food as possible.

GREEN-UP AT CABIN CREEK

When grass sprouts emerge, bears shed the last of their winter lethargy and begin the annual race to consume as much energy-rich food as possible.

Green-up? The process is a familiar one. The snows of winter fade, and in their place, thriving on the meltwater, lush greenery emerges. In the Rocky Mountains the general progression begins at lower elevations and continues through June, July, and into August when spring and fall cojoin in the alpine country. Horsetails, skunk cabbage, young aspen leaves, clover, vetch, lilies in bloom, and especially grasses are critical to bears across the continent during their season of critically lowest energy reserves. This greenery, high in protein and low in cellulose in its early stages, is the primary food of black bears from the time they stumble out of their dens until the berries ripen.

West Yellowstone, Montana, at the base of the Madison Range, is a contemporary trading post where the modern tribes barter their trinkets and totems—bear T-shirts, stuffed bears, bear postcards and belts, and so on. Once significant as the western trailhead into Yellowstone National Park, the town has become an entity unto itself, filled with shops and restaurants, malled and modernized. But at 6667 feet above sea level, West Yellowstone exemplifies the lower level at which green-up begins out here. Take a walk from here up into Cabin Creek at 8,000 feet in the Madison Range, and you pass through two months of green-up.

To take this walk, you resurrect your hiking boots, purchase provisions in West Yellowstone, and overfill the old backpack for a three-day campaign. Escaping back into the hills, you tie off your automobile at the Red Canyon trailhead and walk into a forest of lodgepole pine with an understory thick and junglelike—perfect western black bear habitat. Black bears like thickets for cover and they like to be around water; in general, the wetter the area among western forests, the better the bear habitat.

You pass wild geraniums (white variety) and western thimbleberry (*Rubus parviflorus*) in bloom along the creek. The latter will produce sour little fruits which look like red raspberries and which the bears devour. You notice a tall, hairy herb with a white umbel the size of your hand; this is cow parsnip, *Heracleum lanatum*, a wild parsley, the stems and leaves of which black bears commonly eat. You inspect. No bites evident here.

Onward and upward. Green-up has already passed this lower elevation; the grasses and forbs are brittle with cellulose, but not yet in fruit. Of little value to the bears. You trek back and forth across the narrowing creek, under redstone bluffs, past tiny red side canyons with hairy slopes and moist bottoms. Pausing to admire a rare and delicate yellow columbine, you discover that you are not the first to rest here. Someone has made a bed at the base of a climbable fir next to the trail. In a damp washout a few yards away you find his signature: the perfect print of a large black bear. Wandering down the trail not long ago, pausing along the way for comestibles, he cleared his little nest at the base of this tree. Oval in shape, it measures about two feet by three. One basal branch of the fir has been mangled, some bark torn off. You take your rest by the shady bed, looking for hairs. And find none; but from the looks of it and the track, you realize this bed must be fairly fresh. Suddenly a notion dawns on you. You peer up into the tree. Daybeds or nests like this one are common throughout black bear country. Al LeCount found clusters of them in Arizona, signifying to him consecutive days' use of an area; Gary Alt tracked a Pennsylvania bear which built eight separate nests in two days. Like this one, most nests are located at the base of a tall, straight tree (commonly white pines in the East, assorted conifers and aspens in the West). Black bears like to rest near water, forage, or a large tree.

Nests may be simple raked areas like this one or elaborate in construction. Alt once interrupted a six-year-old male in the process of nest construction. The bear had laid a pile of neatly clipped grass in the nest and covered it with a layer of spruce boughs. All the materials had been gathered within fifty feet of the chosen site. Nearby Alt found two neat sheaves of swamp grass clipped eight to twelve inches long. He has seen beds lined with this type of clipped vegetation before.

Greg Wilker once found a nest lined with a

A sow scrapes moss and other vegetation from the forest floor to prepare a daybed for herself and her cubs at the base of a large pine tree.

flannel shirt—his own. He had left it hanging in a tree while following Number 401 through her routine territory in northeastern Minnesota. When he returned the following day to retrieve it, he found she had incorporated it into her newest daybed. Her two cubs lay asleep on it. He lost his shirt, he'll tell you, to the bears.

But you are not so fortunate. There is no surprise in the crown of the tree today, and you leave with your shirt. You pass an understory thick with highbush huckleberries (*Vaccinium membranaceum*) and grouse whortleberry (*V. scoparium*), both of which will produce summer fruits for the black bears, but which are just in flower at this time. The latter, a tiny little shrub with leaves the size of your smallest fingernail, grows commonly in the shade of lodgepole pines. Feeding on the red berries after months of low rations, black bears pull entire branches through the gap in their teeth, between fang and molar, stripping off all the fruit and half the leaves. Droppings on the trail will tell the story.

You come to a thicker stand of lodgepole pine. One tree next to the trail has been stripped of bark from knee level to over six feet above ground. The huge scar is furrowed with claw marks and covered with sap like candle wax. The picture is coming together now. A male has been here too, likely this spring just prior to mating, to maul this innocent bystanding tree. Stripping bark from trees is a common behavior for the black bear but not likely an expression of territoriality. This marking probably indicates to the available sows that a certain male is in the area and ready for a little action. It may warn off lesser dominant males as well. By rubbing his back against the fresh scar, the male may leave hair and scent for wind dispersal. He possesses no scent gland and must rely on an individual and distinctive body odor designed to identify himself and, perhaps as some believe, to stimulate the sows without cubs to come into season. (Females have been observed rubbing on trees to a lesser extent, but the behavior appears to peak and dissipate by the end of the molt.)

Bears typically mark trees along trails, waterways and ridgetops—their common lanes of travel. They also mark road signs, trail signs, telephone poles, and heavy wooden survey stakes. The marking spots may be traditional, making the chosen trail sign a lost cause for repair. (Marked trees should not be confused with those trees—spruces, firs, and pines—stripped by bears feeding on the inner bark, or cambium. These trees are neatly peeled, often girdled. Significant damage to forests have been reported caused by bears in this fashion in the Pacific Northwest and in northern Montana.) You examine this tree closely, test it for scent. The scar size is typical for black bears, but a black and ungrizzled hair would offer proof. A silver-tipped one, however, would indicate a grizzly was here and make for a better story. You observe three more bear trees in the next quarter mile. All face the trail.

In the meadow on the high divide you find an elk, a young cow, wading belly deep in the dry meadow, grazing. Several hundred yards away, she lifts her muzzle to look your way, then goes back to her forage, changing course slightly in order to avoid you. The meadow is covered in potentilla yellow, lupine blue, the lavender of fireweed and wild open-country geraniums. And that's only what's blooming.

I n a meadow at 9,000 feet you have reached the apex of your journey. Here the grasses are a bit more tender, the flowers younger, many still unopened. Take a moment to rest, put the heavy shirt back on, inspect the territory. Cabin Creek stretches out below. Kirkwood Ridge marches off to your left; Skyline Ridge with White, Redstreak, and Sage Peaks, stands on your right, inviolate as ever.

Carpeting the flanks of these mountains stands a forest of lodgepole pines, Engelmann spruce, and subalpine fir. Bear cover. Along the upper edges of this woodland stand the stoic little whitebark pines—tough as nails, those old trees. High-country acorns to the black bears, the whitebark pine nuts will provide the best fat-producing nutrients available up here in summer. Through the base of the creek valley and scattered on

Bear passersby show great interest in the scents on "bear trees." Even cubs occasionally mark. Telephone poles are favorite "bear" trees. Throughout bear country, telephone poles commonly show teeth marks and wisps of bleaching bear hair.

the hillsides lie the open meadows, still green but, like those you've just crossed, already drying up to cellulose. And off to the northwest stand the craggy Hilgards, still carrying snow. Green-up is still climbing over there; the avalanche chutes glow in pastels of newly sprouted grass.

But with drier grasses here, and the fruits not on yet, what are the bears of this valley eating now? Not much. During this one slack time in the bear's feeding regime, while the grasses harden and the berries sweeten, the black bears take care of that other chore.

The black bear enjoys a much simpler courtship than our own. It moves around freely in perambulatory solitude, spending time only as necessary with mates and family. The only thing it misses, or has failed to acquire, is the joy of bonding between male and female for more than a few conjugal days. In compensation, the black bear has adopted a free and wholesome system of promiscuity in which both males and females may attend to a plurality of mates, different ones on alternate years for the males.

Estrus may last from one to three days in wild Minnesota bears, though captive animals, perhaps due to nutritive levels, have remained in heat for over two weeks. During this period a sow may associate with one male for several days, copulating infrequently, or as Alt observed in Pennsylvania, she may breed with three males within an hour and a half. It appears to be a matter of taste, tolerance, and population density. Breeding with only one mate, or none at all, is likely only where the population is greatly dispersed.

Estrus and mating generally occur in late June and July, but males have associated with females as early as mid-May in Washington State, and estrus has been detected in sows as late as mid-September in the Smokey Mountains. Females nursing six-month-old cubs in July usually fail to come into heat, due to hormonal changes induced by lactation. They will attend their cubs through the summer, den with them (cubs hibernating this time),

and remain as a family the following spring. Shortly thereafter, during that year's mating season, the yearlings leave their mother when she comes into heat and becomes intolerant of them. This general pattern sets up an alternate-year breeding cycle typical of bears in good forage areas. Exceptions, however, must be noted.

Females that lose their newborn cubs by early summer, including zoo animals whose cubs are removed and bottle fed, may breed in successive years. Summertime cub predation or separation may allow a female to come into estrus. Late cub losses may also account for estrus in August and September. Al Erickson removed young cubs from a lactating female in Michigan for two days, during which she bred successfully. In central Arizona, LeCount observed nursing females "dumping" their cubs temporarily and end up producing litters on an annual basis. Alt reported similar cases in Pennsylvania where his sows had cubs one summer and were found in estrus in August while still exhibiting signs of lactation.

Biologists sometimes find that most cubs in a population are born in the same alternate years, an uncommon phenomenon known as "reproductive synchrony." It has been described at various levels of intensity in Pennsylvania, Alberta, and elsewhere. Reproductive synchrony in a black bear population is initiated by a food shortage that results in a general reproductive failure or the loss of most of one year's cubs, initiating synchronized breeding the following year. Synchrony is then maintained when the population's adult females and their female offspring successively breed on the same alternate-year cycle, and it may be further encouraged by an alternate-year "boom and bust" food cycle as found in white oak acorn production. Synchrony is thwarted by inconsistencies in minimum breeding ages, in lengths of breeding cycles and in food availability.

Sexual union between black bears appears impassive and underplayed, much like their aggression. From the journals of a few modern field biologists, we draw a vignette:

Mothers with cubs of the year do not come into estrus and do not mate. Males avoid territories of mothers with young cubs, concentrating instead on territories of mothers that are separating from their seventeen-month-old yearlings as the mothers approach estrus.

131

A male enters a sow's home range, one of seven to fifteen which his intersects (were he in northern Minnesota). In his lust he has avoided the smell and territories of lactating females, concentrating on those in heat. Nose to the ground, he follows the scent trail of this one. For now, the only time in his waking life, his primary goal does not involve foraging. He appears nervous, frantic at times not to lose her trail.

The female knows from the scents on marked trees that he and other males in the area are on the prowl. She is either coming into estrus or there already, and willing to tolerate male presence. Anytime within minutes to a day after the female allows herself to be found, the male responds to some subtle cue—the lay of the sow's ears, perhaps, or the chemistry of her urine. He raises his snout from the ground where she has piddled, licks her face and genitals, and mounts her from behind. He may nip at her ears or hold his head down by her side. Insertion is performed through the employment of a penis bone, or baculum, which, in lieu of blood engorgement, provides erection of his organ.

The male clings to the female, forelegs around her abdomen, thrusting. She stands relatively still, appearing unimpressed. She may walk around, bite off a few stems of grass, look away, or bite at his ears or paws. Both begin to pant, and to quiver a little.

In ten to thirty minutes the process is over, with no copulatory tie as in dogs. The female walks away, hind quarters shaky, apparently tired. The male lies down, sometimes with the female, sometimes cooling himself at streamside.

The sow may copulate on successive days with the same or different males. When she is no longer receptive she will simply move away from her suitors. While she may determine when and how often mating occurs, the choice of mates is not hers. Lynn Rogers describes this process:

"Mating privileges of males appear to be won by contests between males rather than through selection by females. Encounters between mismatched males are settled by the larger ones simply chasing away the smaller, but when contestants are fairly even in size, clawing, biting battles with continuous contact up to four minutes have been seen." It is this rare aggressive contact that provides the scars older males often carry, and which may account for the mangled and broken baculums that Rogers has found on a number of them.

Copulation itself induces ovulation in the female, perhaps a few hours after each encounter, so that cubs of the same litter may have different fathers. This type of reproductive behavior and physiology is genetically advantageous to bear populations as promiscuity and litters of multiple heritage allow enhanced genetic variability of offspring.

At the time of fertilization the sperm and egg combine to form a zygote, which begins to divide and grow. A female may carry from one to as many as six, or possibly more, zygotes. In bears, however, as in opossums and otters and certain rodents, zygote growth stalls at the blastocyst stage when the nascent embryo has developed into a spherical layer of cells resembling a minute raspberry. The blastocysts float freely in the uterus rather than implanting on the uterine wall. This ontogenic suspension, known as "delayed implantation," continues for five months until the approximate time of denning. At that time, if the sow is fat enough (over one hundred and seventy-six pounds, according to Rogers' rule of cub production) the blastocysts will implant and gestation begins. If, however, the sow is starving or too thin (under one hundred and forty-eight pounds), nutrients are partitioned away from the corpus luteum, thereby dropping its production of progesterone, a hormone which supports pregnancy. The blastocysts in a starving bear simply dissolve.

The delayed implantation strategy allows for the survival of a poorly conditioned "almost-pregnant" female which might not have the energy reserves necessary to bear and nurse cubs through the winter. This strategy also lends variability to offspring production and the black bear's reproductive cycle by diminishing successful pregnancies in

This female is rejecting the advances of an amorous male that is turning his head away, signalling nonagression. Females are receptive for one to three days. Copulation lasts from ten to thirty minutes. The most serious fights of the year are between males competing for females. Old males carry many scars from these mating battles.

years of poor food availability.

You hike to the head of Cabin Creek and find your cabin. Someone has nailed barbed wire across the windows. This is bear country. You warm a can of stew over a small fire near the porch. Thunder in the valley. A heavy rain falls. Strobes of lightning illuminate the meadows and ridges in the blue-green electric glare of ancient creation. Pearls of thunder bounce off Echo Peak and rumble up Cabin Creek. God's own incendiaries, these lightning strikes. They'll provide ignition to the dry forest, and there will be more fires in Yellowstone country tomorrow. And therefore, in five, ten, twenty years—depending on the extent and effectiveness of the blazes—woodland openings will regrow, offering grasses and berries and anthills. All part of the scheme.

The rain falls in sheets. The night is magic. Prone to overheating on bright hot days like today, the bears too are cooling off at last.

When western black bears emerge from their dens in early May, they remain sluggish and anorectic for up to two weeks, recovering from the biochemical narcosis of hibernation. Once activated, they may find any of four general food options. The first, the earliest spring vegetation, is a mainstay here as elsewhere on the continent. A second option out here, but of limited availability, is found underground in squirrels' caches of whitebark pine nuts. Rich in fat and protein and highly digestible, pine nuts are an autumn crop and the only counterpart of acorns in the northern Rocky and Sierra Nevada high country. In the fall, black bears may climb for the cones in order to compete with grizzlies, which feed on the nuts only from or beneath ground level. Pine nuts provide critical springtime bear forage only if the previous year's crop was good and the red squirrels did their job.

Carrion is a third option. A fourth spring food alternative for black bears is the outright predation of a living, breathing fawn or calf that it discovers hidden in the grass. Moose, elk, and deer mothers commonly hide their newborn in the very lowland meadows that bears prefer for grazing.

Still, most black bear food studies describe spring food intake as eighty to ninety percent grasses and herbs. Few of these studies have identified all preferred species of grasses and herbs—a difficult task when given only the end product of the process. Such information will become available through the kind of research Rogers is pioneering in Minnesota. Much of the black bears spring diet is also vegetable matter in the forms of roots, corms, early fruits and leaves. Most of the animal fat and protein portion of the bear's diet is of insect origin, usually bees, yellow jackets, ants, and their larvae.

Here at Cabin Creek, green-up begins with glacier lilies (*Erythronium grandflorum*), which emerged in the meadows and blossomed before the snow had all disappeared. Their drooping, pale yellow flowers offer the flavor of fresh cucumbers. Black bears graze on the plants and grizzlies dig the bulbs. In mid-June the spring beauties (*Claytonia lanceolate*) also emerge as bloom and forage. Later you observe the yellow fritillary (*Fritillaria pudica*, also a lily), the shooting star (*Dodecatheon conjugens*), and a host of other blossoms, most of them potential black bear fodder, and many with edible corms or tubers which the black bears may root out.

As the snow recedes, the high country creek beds and seeps green over with stands of grasses and horsetails, soft and fragile to the touch. Green-up proceeds upward in altitude and outward into shaded areas and cooler aspects. Until the huckleberries ripen, the black bears follow the green-up, picking off the occasional aspen leaf or a tender young willow catkin, feeding heavily on lily plants and horsetails.

Why only the newest vegetation? Because at its freshest stage the greenery peaks in protein content. Within days it will harden with cellulose, a structural carbohydrate that remains inert in the bear's gut. The bear's relatively short intestine, remember, was adapted to process large quantities of highly nutritional material at a rapid pace. As a digestive unit, the black bear cannot efficiently

Aspen leaves are a major food in early spring for a couple weeks after the leaf buds burst. Black bears break down saplings to reach the leaves by climbing a tree until it bends, then hanging by their teeth and letting their weight pull the tree down. When other foods are scarce, a bear may break down entire aspen clones.

handle the cellulose-hardened mature vegetation, and therefore must seek the softer tissue.

Even so, the lifesaving green-up is a "negative foraging period" for many black bears, especially nursing mothers. The lushest forbs remain low in energy content, and most bears continue to supplement nutritional needs by using what's left of winter fat stores. During green-up, bears gain structural growth but may lose fat. As a result, they lose weight or gain very slowly. Transition to a positive energy balance generally occurs when the earliest berries become ripe and available.

As green-up passes and reproductive chores are concluded, black bears turn their attention fully to the berries and other soft mast. By August the bears may find strawberries, bearberries, snowberries, red raspberries, and chokecherries. This food group is high in energy, precisely what the bears need to supplement their other foods for weight gain in the long preparation for hibernation. Fattening becomes even more rapid in fall with the availability of hard mast—white bark pine nuts at Canyon Creek, nuts and acorns back east.

These latter diets of soft and hard mast provide proper fodder for the bear's digestive system. Black bears will consume huge quantities of fruits, barely chewing them, to be stored temporarily in the fundus, or anterior section of the stomach, later to be moved aft to the muscular pyloric section which grinds the pits and seeds together to remove the pulp. Because bears do not crush the pits, they avoid the potentially toxic release of cyanogenic material sometimes present in these large, hard seeds. This process also provides for and actually enhances germination of the seeds and pits after dispersal and disposal by the wandering bruins. The grizzly thus takes responsibility for the success of the cow parsnip, the black bear for many others including the wild plum, for which it is one of the few vehicles of long-range dispersal.

While the green-up generally progresses upward in altitude and fruit production is earliest and heaviest down in the canyons, this does not indicate a general cyclical migration for black bears. Each one moves around in its home range and on feeding forays as necessary and convenient.

Cubs are the exceptions to the black bears negative springtime growth curve. With an average weight of from four to eight pounds when they leave their dens, these youngsters must grow and lay on enough fat to survive hibernation, only five months away. Much of their early weight gain occurs through nursing, at the expense of the mother. Milk remains their primary food through early June. In prime Montana habitat, Jonkel and Cowan found cubs averaging thirty pounds by August, when weaning begins, and forty pounds just prior to denning. In Pennsylvania cubs grow to as much as seventy-six pounds, and in a few cases over one hundred pounds, prior to their first hibernation, but growth there represents about twice the continental average.

Small yearlings may nurse during early spring months, and may, again particularly in the West and northern parts of their range, remain with the mother through the entire second summer, lengthening her breeding cycle to three years. Individual cubs have proven themselves self-sufficient, however, by the age of five and a half months and weighing as little as eight pounds.

Sows are protective parents, sending their cubs up a tree at the sign of danger as early as the first day out of the den. They teach foraging by example, and sometimes lead the cubs to distant feeding areas to which the cubs may return, years later, by themselves. Discipline may be strict but appears balanced in noncritical circumstances by much tolerance and restraint (like that exhibited toward humans). Cubs, in turn, seem to listen well and follow the subtlest directions.

The relationship between weight gain and habitat quality deserves one further note. Weight loss or gain in black bears varies, as always, with relative abundance and availability of foods, which in turn varies from year to year, drainage to drainage, and across the continent. One expects a black bear in

Mothers prefer to park their cubs at the bases of large trees with solid, easy-to-climb bark. Cubs commonly fall from trees with slippery or shaggy bark. This cub cries for help during its first climb and is being rescued by the mother. She carried it down.

Pennsylvania or southern Quebec to be lightest a month after den emergence, and to gain weight slowly through green-up until proteins and fats are deposited at higher rates when mast crops are available. Bears in habitats of lesser quality are more likely to continue to lose weight through June and July. But the difference in rate of weight gain or loss is not proportional to the caloric intake of foods, because energy intake fulfills body maintenance needs first and growth or weight gain second. Let us assume, for example, that a two hundred pound black bear requires 2,000 kilocalories of energy intake to break even in metabolic needs and body maintenance. If this bear consumes 2,100 kilocalories on a given day, one hundred kilocalories would be available for growth. In slightly better habitat, the same bear eats 2,200 kilocalories in a day, thereby providing two hundred kilocalories for growth. Thus, in our oversimplified and hypothetical case, an increase in habitat quality (measured in caloric units) of less than five percent has doubled the animal's weight gain.

A pattern emerges here. Springtime or green-up is a critical survival period for black bears across the continent, we know. But it may be even more important to black bears of the West and much of Canada where berries ripen later in summer and hard masts are much less available in the fall. Prolonged, and perhaps lusher in areas of late snowmelt, the green-up becomes a larger fraction of the black bear's summer diet. In these areas, which happen to offer more grasslands and fewer human-raised crops for emergency rations, the green-up may be just as important to bear survival and production as the autumn mast crops are elsewhere.

Despite continued increases in human encroachment, black bear habitat in Montana may be improving, according to Dennis Flath, a biologist for Montana Department of Fish, Wildlife and Parks in Bozeman. Logging for railroad ties, mine timbers, and sawlogs after the turn of the century probably enhanced black bear habitat by creating openings in the forest. Problems began in the forties when foresters perceived the need for reforestation, and responded to it with monoculture management: pure stands of single species, all planted at once, a wholly unnatural alternative to the natural mosaics. Next came an era of clearcutting that erased black bear habitat but eventually ushered in a new conscience and appreciation for natural dispersion. With that in mind, management today is righting the old wrongs, to some extent, and improving the forest cover for bears.

Another factor in Montana's black bear equation is the evolution of human attitudes toward bears. While bear-human conflicts increase with the number of humans living and playing in bear country, in the past twenty-five years the black bear has risen in perceived value from bountied vermin to a treasured big game animal. Where a few mountain men and a few thousand Indians pursued the black bear for food and fur a century and a half ago, nearly 50,000 black bear hunters killed over 1,200 bears last year in Montana. The black bear is now the fourth most popular game animal in the state, following deer, elk, and antelope. Hunter pressure steadily increases. In a few areas, the Cabinet Range for example, the harvested bears are getting smaller each year. Due to an extensive system of logging roads, the area is threatened with overhunting.

Biologists and game managers here hold the responsibility for the health and size of the bear population, but little authority over habitat loss and degradation. They concentrate on regulation of the harvest and have turned to a quota system in certain areas: The season in a given unit closes as soon as a prescribed number of bears (or of sows) has been killed. Osborne Russell killed his bears out under the big sky with great freedom and little concern except for a clean kill and the time to skin out the carcass before the Crows or Old Ephraim (the grizz) discovered him. The modern hunter, in his or her attempt to relive in some fashion that atavistic freedom, must first study numerous pages of fine newsprint constituting the black bear hunting regulations for Big Sky Country. One more technocratic bite out of the wilderness experience.

Mothers lead their cubs to feeding areas which the cubs remember, returning to places their mothers showed them many miles outside their territories.

"We've undertaken more black bear management in the last five years than in the fifty before that," Flath told me. Is it enough? Probably so. For now, anyway. His department, unlike many state fish and game agencies, has the budget and personnel to support good management. Good management? Black bear management in Montana, another biologist told me, is thirty years behind deer management.

With the closure of garbage dumps and the dramatic increase in the elk population, the grizzlies of the Yellowstone ecosystem have apparently, and in general, become more predacious. There are observations and evidence of an increase in the number of elk killed by grizzlies. And not just calves, but mature adults as well, from spring into autumn.

Can a black bear kill a full-grown elk? Yellowstone wildlife biologist Doug Huston can answer that. Last May, while flying an elk census over the park, he watched a black bear drive a mature bull into deep snow and kill it.

Might the local black bear population also become more predacious on this bonanza of elk? It would be possible, of course, to some extent. But the black bear is not the predator that the dominant and overtempered grizzly is. Then again, the black bear is an intelligent and resourceful animal known for its unique behavioral traits. If the pine nuts fail or the berry crop dries up one year, we might expect a few more black bears to chase down elk.

Although they may be seen taking elk now and then, black bear sightings in this country are not all that common. The grizzly bear is generally a larger and stronger bear of standard and hasty malcontent. With the exception of man, the grizzly is master of these meadows and, therefore, to be avoided. Black bear sows with young cubs are particularly shy about leaving forest cover under daylight in grizzly or human country. The solitary nature of the black bear, roaming alone or in small family groups in forested areas, renders it less visible.

A related consideration is the population density of black bears here: the dispersion of so few individuals across so much country. Montana game biologists estimate a black bear density of just over one bear per square mile in the best habitats, less than that in forested country elsewhere in the state. Biologist in Yellowstone found 0.7 bears per square mile in the best bear country there, 0.2 parkwide. (Yellowstone is marginal bear habitat anyway, particularly since the dumps and feeding stations have been closed.)

But population densities of black bears are dubious statistics, impossible to certify, difficult even to estimate. Few of the tricks and techniques biologists usually employ to measure wild animal populations work well with black bears. Census from ground or air is impossible due to the retiring nature of the species and its affinity for the thick bush. The numbers of bears seen by hikers, homeowners, dump operators, campers, sheepherders and other observers, as well as the numbers killed by hunters and traffic, vary more according to how much the bears are traveling at the time, due to food availability, than to how many bears exist in the area. The same bias afflicts the use of bait or scent stations—lures set out at regular intervals, each surrounded by a patch of raked soil in which the tracks of visiting bears may be counted. Some of the best estimates come from trapping and marking efforts. Eventually, when all the bears trapped already wear tags, you may assume you have counted most of the bears in your study area, but unless the bears were given radio-collars, it is impossible to tell how many of them were just passing through, inflating the count.

Population density estimates are too imprecise for exact comparisons but may offer a gross comparison of populations and habitat qualities. Densities range from highs of eight to ten bears per square mile in certain parts of Alaska (apparently during concentrations at a rare fishing site) and Pennsylvania; to four per square mile on a repopulated island of good habitat off the coast of Washington; to levels of about one bear per square mile in northern California, northern Maine, the bear

Wolf-killed moose or deer are occasional sources of protein. Pupae are found in clusters that can make ant-eating efficient. The pupae are higher in fat than the adult ant and do not spray formic acid. There are few locations where black bears can easily catch spawning fish. Fish are at best a minor food item for most black bears.

habitat of Arizona, the rest of Washington State, some of Montana, much of Alberta, much of the Great Smokeys; and down to about half that in northern Minnesota, Michigan, and the still re-expanding population in Massachusetts. From this glance, we may generalize that in areas of "good" black bear habitat we might expect one or more bears per square mile. In areas of concentrations of extremely good habitat we expect three to ten per square mile. And in marginal areas, perhaps one-half bear per square mile. No one, it appears, has reported a black bear population density of less than one bear in ten square miles. We may tentatively conclude from this that below that density black bears cannot function as a population. They would have to spend too much energy in traveling to find food in the sub-marginal land, or their chances of mating encounters would be so diminished as to preclude a regenerative level of sexual interaction.

Black bear distribution may be determined by another factor: heat. Bears are an evolutionary product of the cold woods; they are adapted to a harsh cold season but have not provided themselves with an efficient heat exchange system which would allow them to dissipate the noon heat of a July day above eighty degrees Fahrenheit. Black bears in particular, with their heat-absorbing black fur, remain in the shady woods, find water, and resist exercise to avoid heat stress. The more variable and lighter colors of fur on western black bears—chocolate through cinnamon to blond—may be a genetic adaptation to reflect more solar radiation in a landscape which offers less shade. Still, at least half of the black bears in this area are black, and even those sporting lighter shades must suffer under their heavy coats.

Under the heat of clear summer days, then, it is not unusual for the bears to remain in cover, unseen. Even in good bear country, the biologist must park his pickup and go look for them.

The elusive black bear is difficult to census. Most census techniques rely on baiting, so results reflect bear hunger as much as bear numbers.

In grizzly country, black bears avoid open areas. After grizzly bears disappeared from the open tundra of northern Labrador, black bears extended their range and now live hundreds of miles from forest cover.

143

CHAPTER 8

WALKING WITH THE BEARS

"But if we are going to learn more about animals—real knowledge, not more facts—we are going to have to get out into the woods."

— Barry Lopez, in *Of Wolves and Men*

A Day in the Life: May 25

08:42—In the midst of usual morning operations here in the bush at the southern edge of the Canadian Shield, a silence blooms. The timid thrushes stop their fluting. A gray jay freezes in his thieving tracks. Even the long-winded winter wrens shut their bills. Nothing speaks except for one apprehensive red squirrel and the standard pair of trouble-loving ravens, croaking and clanking from their aerial advantage. Several aspens begin to tremble.

Down in the alders by the head of Keeley Creek, a tributary of the Kawishiwi, something sizeable but ungainly corrupts the morning peace.

On a small aspen- and birch-covered upland nearby, one black bear has halted, head upraised, ears alert and forward, nose in the wind. There is a look of intensity on its ursine face. She's heard this kind of thrashing before, may even recognize it. Still, relying first on an instinctive reaction to the squirrel chatter and the quiet in the woods, she blows out two loud woofs, and from within yards of her a pair of black cubs, maybe eight pounds apiece, bolt up a large aspen. They scale its rough lower bark with ease, freestyle, and stop in the canopy to yawn and sniff the air.

The intruder approaches, crashing through the brush like an injured animal. Or maddened. The bear rises to sniff again, then watches.

Twenty yards away a young male, about one hundred and eighty pounds—nearly forty pounds heavier than the sow— steps into view. Rather lanky and rugged looking, with short brown hair and a resolute but patient visage, he watches her for a reaction. Neither injured nor mad, he does suffer one major affliction, which the female perceived much earlier: He is human.

One of the humans, in fact, that she has observed on many occasions now. She has monitored his behavior, scent, and apparent intentions. According to her experience, he offers no threat. Her natural fear of humans has dissolved, or at least for this particular individual and two or three others, into a mild watchfulness and sometimes complete inattention to their presence.

The bear recognizes the young man as an individual and unique organism, defined by peculiar scent and physical attributes. She has no need of mnemonic devices with which to label him. The human, on the other hand, is an animal dependent upon devices of notation and secondary representation. He has both a number and a name for this bear as well as for himself. He is Greg Wilker, biological technician, field assistant, and bear man.

His assignment for the next twenty-four hours, if all goes well, is to follow the bear family, recording at close range every bite taken, every drink drunk, every behavior performed. He carries no weapon, no dart gun, and no food which might bias the bears' behavior. He is outfitted only with a portable computer, eyes, and patience.

08:56—Satisfied and relaxed, the sow defecates, an initial data point for the young biologist, and walks away.

This proves interesting, of course, to Wilker. Nothing like a fresh turd to excite the instincts and gladden the heart of the field biologist. He examines it closely for form and content, finding it more interesting than expected: The dropping is green, foul smelling, semi-liquid, and contains the hoof of a fawn. A rare find, since most droppings of digested animal flesh wash away or disintegrate before they are found. Scats are counted and collected by wildlife biologists to identify species, infer population numbers, and analyze diets. Those dropped by bears feeding on vegetation generally last longer, are more likely found, and may, Wilker is thinking, bias food studies.

(Next to carrion, a fawn is the most likely venison afforded to a black bear, but there is no proof

Greg Wilker shows Patch the computer he will use to record her every action, bite of food, and habitat use. Black bear habitat studies at the North Central Forest Experiment Station involve walking, resting, and sleeping with wild, habituated black bears for twenty-four to forty-eight hours at a time. The detailed information allows forest managers to make decisions that can help bears.

here of predation. The bear may have found it stillborn or the result of a wolf or road kill.)

08:58—The adult bear climbs the aspen to her cubs, then returns to the ground.

09:02—Rotating her head toward Wilker, then away, our primary subject grunts quietly, then sits human-like, butt on the ground and back against a small jack pine. The cubs scramble down their tree, descending in upright fashion like painters coming down a ladder. They move immediately to mother and begin to nurse, emitting a vibrato hum. Together they sound to Wilker like a small flock of cooing pigeons. After three minutes they become quiet and nurse for another minute and a half, at which point the sow brushes them aside, stands, walks away.

09:12—Still walking, cubs in tow. The adult bear plods along in steady ambulation—left front, right rear, right front, left rear, ad libitum, breaking stride only to sniff ground, vegetation, and air here and there, taking the occasional bit of something and moving on while chewing. She takes her direction from various inputs registered through nose, ears, eyes, seemingly in that order. It is a smooth movement over and through irregular terrain, a graceful and sensitive gait, gentle, rolling, and highly toned. Absolutely silent for the most part.

Wilker tramps along behind, pausing to enter notes into the computer.

09:15—Both cubs have been staying within ten to fifteen yards of their mother. The biologist has found himself closer to her than them on more than one occasion already. Now one cub, having dropped behind, cries. The sibling, also crying, runs back to his sister. The sow watches, allows them to catch up, walks on.

09:16—Bear sits down. Cubs playing nearby. Wilker stands and waits.

09:18—Wilker sits down.

09:19—Bear up and meandering again. Not meandering in the sense of confusion, but taking a wide latitude of digressions along a straight or curvilinear trail of obvious intent. Looking, finding, testing, probably recognizing and memorizing much as she tromps along, planting her plantigrade paws firmly and surely on the earth, exorcising the flavor and juices from a bite of grass in free and open-mouthed fashion as she walks along.

09:24—Sits again. Contemplating. Perhaps contemplating Wilker. She glances at the biologist, reminding him to make his computer entry. He does so, noting their passage through a damp open lowland of mosses, leatherleaf, bog laurel, and the insect-trapping pitcher plant. This lowland is reminiscent of the tundra plains five hundred miles to the north. A microcosmic approximation of interior grizzly country.

09:25—She moves on, climbing the next rise, holding a general westward course. Whatever the mother sniffs at, the cubs sniff too. When intent on olfaction, the sow raises her snout, drops her lower jaw, and laps at the air while inhaling. The sound produced is not a snort but a mild, abbreviated snore, like the sinal sniffing of an old hound picking up a trail. In doing so she employs the rudimentary vomeronasal, or Jacobson's, organ (highly developed in and used by snakes and lizards) in her palate to enhance her perception of airborne spores.

09:42—First serious feeding noted. Sow takes several bites of large-leafed aster (*Aster macrophyllus*), passing up the tender fiddleheads of an interrupted fern immediately next to it.

Wilker stays within fifteen or twenty feet of the bear, particularly while she eats, in order to identify food items and count bites. Last August he tracked this same bear across twenty-two miles to a hazelnut stand near Greenwood Lake, the destination of her "fall shuffle." The following day she employed herself full-time, attended by Wilker

and his computer, digging up squirrel middens to consume cached hazelnuts and pick freshly dehisced nuts off the ground. She found the general location of each midden by sniffing the air, the specific by mashing her nose to the ground. She'll find ant nests this June in the same fashion.

The nuts she picked up one by one between tongue and extended upper lip, transferred each to the rear of her mouth, cracked it, and chewed it carefully, discarding hull fragments out the front and sides of her mouth. Sometimes while chewing she allowed chunks of the meat to fall onto the back of a forepaw for later retrieval.

Stopping only to sleep, she swallowed 2605, or nearly seven pounds of hazelnuts that day, about one every twenty seconds while awake.

09:43—The cubs bite the aster too, mouthing it like their mother. Wilker is uncertain that they swallow any of it. In any case, using only her example and the cubs' innate curiosity, the bear mother teaches her offspring something about food selection. She feeds; they play and mimic. An innocent, idyllic education.

09:46—Leave asters.

09:51—Begin more serious feeding among rock outcrops in mixed northern forest type. Cubs climb a ten-inch cedar and fall asleep. Sow takes two hundred twenty-seven bites of peavine (*Lathyrus spp.*), a vetch-like legume growing here in shallow, poor soils on top of the oldest rock formation on the continent. The biologist takes a few bite-size samples himself in order to determine, back at the lab, how much the bear has eaten.

For twenty minutes the sow alternates feeding with sitting quietly. She takes two hundred fourteen additional bites of peavine.

The bear eats vetch, grass, and clover in much the same way that it picks and eats berries. The morsel is grasped behind the incisors, plucked with a pull of the head, and swallowed. Grasses are chewed more thoroughly than mast and manipulated frequently by tongue. The combination of excellent sense of smell, good close-range vision, and dexterity of lips, tongue, and claws renders the bear surprisingly clean and delicate in its feeding.

10:11—Sow moves on, ignoring cubs, who watch from tree top.

10:14—Seven bites of young aspen leaves. Cubs descend pine and follow.

10:30—Sow takes break from peavine (two hundred three bites) for a three-second drink. One cub attempts to follow suit, inhales at wrong time, snorts, sneezes, retreats from the hazard.

10:31—While Wilker punches data into the computer, the bear glances back toward him, checking his progress, monitoring his behavior, curious that this animal never eats.

10:34—The family moves into a berry patch from which they will harvest blueberries later this summer. Today, however, they eat only the flowers of the bear berry (*Arctostaphylos uva-ursi*), selecting them carefully and not touching the blueberry blossoms.

10:40—The sow urinates just enough to soak her long vulval hairs. Then with obvious intent she straddles a six-foot aspen, forcing its trembling foliage between her forelegs and dragging it against her moisture. Wilker notices the pattern, observes the pungency, makes an entry on the computer. It seems very likely from his observations that female black bears regulate urine flow, painting a scent cover over their territories. Evidence for active territorialism among sows, these observations may add a new shape, a realistic perimeter, to current home range studies.

10:49—Into and out of another wet lowland, Wilker follows the bears. As always, he hopes to see

As the female walked about her territory, she straddled occasional saplings to scent-mark them with urine.

some dramatic spectacle, some predaceous move by the animal mother. A silent stalk, the sudden kill, the bloody feast—something to remember, a story to tell back at the lab and on Saturday evening at the North Country Saloon over in Ely. A touch of carnivorous romance. The timeless carnal thrill. Is that too much to ask? Yet what he sees in the bear before him is an easygoing vegetarian pacifist. The pitcher plants, even in their rooted, vegetative condition, are more truly carnivorous than the carnivore pacing ahead.

10:52—Climb to another upland. The bears of Quetico country have no mountains to go over. They see what they can see from inferior vantage points on low inclines, rocky outcrops, moss-covered ledges. They use their noses a lot, and appear satisfied with their mild topography. As long as there's something to eat.

Under a mixed canopy of aspen, spruce, birch, and pine the bears find more peavine. Twenty-eight bites here, thirty there. Eat and walk. Walk and sniff and eat. Slow and steady fattens the bear. Or keeps it alive. At this point in the springtime, before the berries are ripe with carbohydrates, an adult bear is still losing weight. Particularly a nursing female. She feeds only to lessen her energy drain, still living in part off the little remaining fat laid on for last winter.

11:12—The bear mother sits to nurse the young. She ignores Wilker. Listening to the cubs' security song, Wilker can discern two distinct voices. Researchers elsewhere listen at dens in March to predict litter size.

11:16—Finished nursing, the sow sits quietly for a minute. The cubs appear restless and playful, as usual, after their meal. They shamble off, according to habit, to relieve themselves.

11:18—Trail is resumed; the she-bear is back into the peavine, sitting to eat in restful fashion, then walking to the next patch. Her pubic hairs, Wilker notes, are dry now.

12:13—Nineteen bites of wild calla (*Calla palustris*) at the edge of another boggy opening. Crotch wet again, the sow labels the shrubbery upon entering and exiting the wetland. In the center she finds water, takes a long drink, keeps moving. Even in May the direct sunlight can overheat a black creature under a heavy fur coat.

12:28—While their mother consumes peavine (seventy-eight bites by Wilker's count, and he's close enough to count her teeth) the cubs ascend a ten-inch cedar and fall asleep, draped across separate limbs.

12:35—Primary subject drops Wilker another data point. Green and very wet again, containing more deer parts.

12:36—Roughage for the constitution: one hundred and twenty-one bites of peavine.

12:47—Cubs still in tree; mother throws her bulk down (literally) to rest, but her head and ears remain erect and alert. Wilker notes that while the bears are continuous feeders, they appear for the most part nonchalant about it. They spend half their time standing at ease, sitting, or lying to rest. If—as some believe— the black bear is off its guard when eating, Wilker sees them constantly taking stock of the spectrum of environmental cues while resting and walking.

13:03—Walking slowly, harvesting peavine (two hundred and eighteen bites).

13:18—Wandering slowly, still in vicinity of cubs, but now close to Highway 1. Spotted by pickup truck, which blows siren. Bear runs to cubs' tree, grunting, and sits down. Truck fails to stop.

13:23—Perceived threat is gone. Bear falls to one side, ears still erect.

13:25—Rolls to belly, head on crossed

forepaws. Wilker wishes he had brought his six-pound camera after all. Ears sag (the bear's), muscles relax. Still not asleep, though.

She may remain more alert due to the cubs, thinks the biologist. Last year this bear typically sought out a dense thicket of spruce or fir, secreted herself within, and slept soundly through the heat of midday.

13:27—Cubs sense opportunity, come down on their own and begin to nurse on the recumbent mother, humming at first, then quiescent.

13:32—Mother sits up, listening intently. A woodpecker drums—pileated, Wilker thinks. Cubs walk around, successfully complete traditional post-feeding chores, reascend tree.

13:34—Forest sounds ebbing in the warmth of midday; bear mother drifts off to sleep.

14:54—Something in her ear pricks her awake. She lies alert. Wilker listens, hears nothing.

14:58—She yawns, scratches her muzzle with a hind paw, doglike, and arises.

14:59—Urinates (four seconds) and defecates, and watches the biological inspection. Still loose from the venison, but no deer parts. Wilker describes the commodity in detail on his computer.

15:01—Wilker and bear stretch legs independently. Bear emits low moans toward cubs.

15:08—Nursing, usual procedure.

15:13—Family strikes camp, moves on.

15:19—Bear stalks innocent victim, descending on it with jaws open: eight bites of peavine.

15:20—Ears alert again, still hearing some-

thing. Again Wilker listens, but hears only the crescendo of insect wings. Tiny, but fearsome in number. Could be a long night, he thinks. Long and parasitic. (He's been here before.)

15:25—At a woodland pond our bear takes a long drink, nine seconds in duration, then wades in. She immerses her muzzle up to the eye sockets, apparently not to drink but to cool off. Then blots water onto the top of her head with her left paw, not once but several times. Wilker enters data madly, quite aware that no one relying solely on telemmetry signals makes this kind of observation.

15:35—Bear is walking, sniffing ground, ears alert again. Cubs, having survived another introduction to the aquatic world, come running back to mother, brushing past the invisible biologist in the process.

15:39—Bear sets her ears. Wilker hears it this time—a red-tailed hawk is calling nearby. The adult bear has already bolted toward the screaming, leaving cubs and biologist to catch up.

15:41—The hawk soars in large, low circles, calling. The bear follows these screams, which to the biologist sound remarkably similar to cub distress calls. Wilker plumbs the possibilities.

15:49—Back with cubs, feeding again. Ninety-nine bites of peavine and counting.

16:13—Bear and cubs cross Highway 1, amble up a grassy woods road, and begin feeding on clover (*Trifolium spp.*), dandelion (*Taraxacum officinale*), and some grasses along the dirt lane. They move in and out of the forest edge along the road. Wet again, the she-bear paints her territory.

17:09—Still working their way along, feeding, courtesy of the U.S. Forest Service road engineers. Busy fellows. Another small freshet, another drink.

17:10—Weaving back to the edge of Highway 1. Wilker grows nervous at the idea that his bear and her cubs gamble for their grass by the big road, however light the traffic might be. Grass, dandelion, peavine—two hundred and thirty-nine bites. The hum in the understory builds—that enervating, torturing promise of another bloody feast—the ominous whine of ten billion hungry little hypodermic-nosed arthropods, armed and ready for the gang wars of survival. Wilker enters data with pluck. He'll be fighting for his corpuscles tonight.

17:29—Car approaching on highway. Bear hears it before Wilker.

17:30—Distinguished gray late-model Buick with out-of-state tags (dangerous in any state) vectors by, cruising northwesterly at seventy-four in a fifty-five zone. In their climate-controlled environment behind tinted glass, the inhabitants—a professional couple, fortyish, from a suburb of Chicago—are absorbed in their normal heated conversation. They are on vacation, after all. They fail to see the bear, the beautiful boreal countryside, the Minnesota state trooper standing in ambush by the Kawishiwi River bridge. Ever wary of Buicks, however, the bear takes two quick steps into the woods, toward her cubs, watches the merry couple motor past, then returns to the open grass to feed. Wilker follows.

17:40—Back into the woods with cubs and biologist in tow. Wandering cross-country in serendipitous fashion, it might appear, but Wilker knows otherwise. As casually as his bears seem to choose their trails, they arrive too often at traditional feeding areas, old daybeds, piles of composting bear scat which they invariable augment with freshly prepared stock. These bears know their entire ranges, Wilker feels, and reckon their meanderings more than is readily apparent. They move across the land with great sensitivity, continually updating and upgrading this knowledge.

17:14—Onto another grassy woods road. The insects are on patrol now, growing fierce. The excitement of following a large carnivore Dian Fossey-style wears a little thinner, Wilker notices, after four thousand bites of peavine by the bear and two hundred of Wilker by the insolent, obtrusive mosquitoes.

Men go mad under these conditions, thinks Wilker, but he's been through this before, and wouldn't think of losing his cool in the presence of the bears. Instead, he rubs the little bastards out, brushes them away. Those that he can reach. The rest of them he continues to feed, in silence but under protest. He watches his bear for a reaction to the swarming devils, but sees something else instead.

17:56—Near the edge of a thick alder swamp the she-bear suddenly stiffens her gait and woofs to the cubs, who immediately scramble up the rough bark of a large white pine. The bear sniffs, wags her head, stands erect on her hind legs, ears up, round and forward like radar dishes, her nose flanged like a hog's snout. Then down to all fours, trotting almost, with front shoulders bouncing, toward the alders. Wilker senses the strong essence of urine. In an instant the sow explodes into a fluid sprint, ears back and head down, but just as suddenly she breaks off the charge, slamming her forepaws to the earth with a force Wilker can feel twenty yards away. Something large and bear-like moves away through the alders.

The territorial black bear mother is a quick and fearsome beast, but immediately upon termination of her bluff she turns with extreme nonchalance and peacefulness to wander back toward Wilker and her cubs, biting off a nip of peavine en route. All aggression disappeared the instant she quit the charge. She calls her cubs down, and as she turns to resume feeding operations, Wilker notices that her entire groin and the inner side of each thigh are soaked with urine.

18:15—Two hundred and seven bites of peavine.

18:29—Sows pauses at five-inch aspen log on ground, sniffs at it, decides to dig. Holding down the log with a heavy right forepaw, she uses her left to rake vigorously with her strong, recurved claws. The action appears aggressive, vengeful, as she employs her powerful musculature to tear into the wood fiber. She stops to sniff. Too early for ants, but the potential was tested nevertheless. Satisfied, she moves along. One of the cubs scratches where she did, extracts a few splinters, bites the log and bounces back to join mother.

That same paw which can tear apart solid wood also affords its owner a partial and powerful but delicate grasp. Not blessed with an opposable thumb—the bear's big toes are all on the wrong side, the outside, of its feet—a black bear can articulate the claw tips of its forefoot toward the front pad to grip, for example, branches when feeding on berries. Forepaws with claws straightened (they are not retractable) are used to dig, rake grass and leaf litter, and in the same motion, always toward the body, to grasp the far side of a rock or log and turn it over in search of insects. The other major use of the claws is climbing, not predation, though she may use her paws to swat at or trap small prey against the ground. The skin of her pads is a sensitive organ. A rough callous is shed from it each year in the den, leaving a soft, supple new pad which may bleed when first walked on.

18:31—Bear pauses in a rump-high stand of young aspens. The evening sunlight filtering obliquely through a canopy of newly unfurled leaves reflects lime green in the sheen of her coat. Wilker entertains a poetic thought. A breeze moves through. The quakies quake. Under this pattern of shimmer and shadow the one hundred and forty-pound bear is difficult to see, almost invisible. Only her large, round ears would give her away to Wilker's eye, had he not followed her here.

Those ears, employed here in the aspen chatter to amplify directional hearing, are also a chief means of gesticular communication. While early naturalists perceived bears as solitary and asocial, animal behaviorists now recognize bears as highly social animals of subtle communication technique. Wilker watches these large ears (larger and rounder than the grizzly's). Erect and forward they signify alertness, anticipation. Held laterally: relaxed or playful. Partially flattened: threat reaction. And fully flattened to the neck: defense or aggression, which may be further communicated in the form of a bluff—a more direct and emphatic gesture.

18:34—Sow bounds up an eight-inch aspen to sample fresh leaves. Forty bites in all. Cubs remain on ground. Play initiates by means of a bite, remains quiet until one cub bawls, ready to quit.

18:35—Sow returns to cubs. Wilker quietly dispatches a mosquito, inspects his quarry.

18:36—Cross another wetland and back into the woods. With the exceptions of the woods road meanders, the bear has led her little band almost constantly westward through the day.

18:36—Attending motherly duties.

18:53—Another grassy road, another four hundred and forty-two bites of clover. For the next hour our little research caravan moves slowly westward, the adult female feasting on clover, over 1,000 bites, and her cubs mouthing it, appearing to swallow some of the leaves. Wilker, of course, is fasting today, consuming only bits of information and various but important internal impressions. And donating heavily to the insect drive.

19:31—Sharp pain in the calf of Wilker's right leg. The cubs had been playing hard together when one of them lit out toward Wilker, bit him on the calf, and ran back to her sibling, by way of mother, to continue the vigorous play. An invitation, perhaps?

Snatching a dandelion green from a forest road.

19:50—Still mowing the clover.

20:26—Back into the mixed forest. Cooler now, and almost dark.

20:44—Bear sits down.

20:45—Scratches ear, then chin.

20:46—Defecates. Same old data, interpreted under a flashlight beam.

20:47—Walking and feeding.

21:01—Seventy-six bites of peavine.

21:31—Sow sits and nurses cubs, which appear tired.

21:37—Sow curls up on side in fetal position; cubs lie next to her in small depression at base of large white pine, the escape tree.

21:44—All bears asleep. Wilker is lying down too, resting fitfully but not asleep.

23:58—Bear mother rolls to other side. Wilker moves quietly off anthill.

00:06 (six minutes after midnight)—Sow nurses cubs.

05:45—Nursing again.

05:52—Bear sits up and yawns. Wilker yawns.

05:53—Wilker scratches shanks, bear scratches side against tree. Look at each other, shake their heads.

06:05—Cubs climb tree, then descend. Family gets underway.

06:22—Back to grassy lane to feed on clover.

06:49—Bear family wanders into an upland clearcut, but not far into the open. The bolder males may feed clear to the center of a medium-sized clearing on a cool day when the berries are ripe, but females, particularly those with cubs, remain in the safety of the margins.

07:26—Back into the peavine habit—fifty bites.

08:09—Sow sits; cubs nurse.

08:20—Sow takes four-minute rest period, forcing same on cubs.

08:35—Bears intersect yet another woods road, heading ever westward across this rugged, glaciated terrain, the sow's home ground. Along the road edge the sow straddles innocent young balsams and poplars, drizzling her scent.

08:36—Three hundred and nine bites of clover.

08:53—Eighty-seven bites of clover. Cubs appear intent on their own feeding behavior.

During the past day the female has been actively feeding for nearly one-third of her time awake, taking primarily clover from the road openings and peavine in the upland woods. A fairly constant diet of one or two major food items is not unusual for a day in the life of any of Wilker's bears. Which items taken, however, depends on the season, the habitat in which the bear ranges, and perhaps the bear itself. At least in the spring, however, that typical food species that is most abundant is usually the primary course. On this same day another bear whose territory might encompass primarily ash swamps would eat mostly grasses, the typical understory of that type of habitat. A day in mid-June would likely find either bear eating the pupae from

Crossing the highway is a nervous event for Patch and her cubs. She looks, listens, and then hurries across, grunting to the cubs with special urgency.

ant nests. In August, hazelnuts. In October, acorns, where available. In general, that food which avails the highest energy content and digestibility.

The sow has spent another third of her time wandering afoot, often feeding intermittently in the process. She has slept and rested for over nine hours. She invested only forty-five minutes in the nursing of her cubs.

Nearly half of her time was spent along the edge of an upland clearcut, sleeping the night there, and a third of it under the cover of the mixed boreal upland forest, the predominant habitat type of her territory. She spent almost three and a half hours on woods roads, walking, resting, feeding on clover.

08:56—Sitting in her morning clover, three miles from the aspens under which Wilker found her one day ago, the sow attempts to extract a leaf flattened to the roof of her mouth. Finishing, she raises her gaze, cups her ears, looks around. She and her family are quite alone. Eager to depart the bush with his computer full of notes and what's left of his plasma content, the biologist has suddenly disappeared.

Author's note: The preceding account was derived largely from a day in the life of the bear named Patch and the technician named Greg Wilker, both of whom were then under the supervision of Dr. Lynn Rogers of North Central Forest Experiment Station. At this writing, Lynn, Greg, and two other technicians have walked (and slept) with five different bears during thirty-one separate twenty-four hour encounters.

MULTIPLE USE
SUPERIOR NATIONAL FOREST

FISHING   POWER   PLANTATION

HIGHWAY NO. 1

CAMPGROUND   TRUCK TRAIL   LOGGIN

RIVER

RESEARCH   HUNTING

KAWISHIWI

FORAGE

RECREATION WATER

CHAPTER 9

THE INFLUENCE OF MODERN MAN

As people increase in number and make more demands upon the forest, conflicts between human needs and wildlife habitat needs will increase. It will become increasingly important for forest managers to know the needs of wildlife in order to maintain viable wildlife populations. Wide-ranging species like black bears are among the animals most threatened when forests are converted to human use.

"**I**n a war among the races," John Muir wrote somewhere, "I would side with the bears." Interesting, his use of the word "races." As for the term war, we understand that meaning all too clearly. Peter Matthiessen defined it best thirty years ago in his *Wildlife in America* as "the white man's war of attrition against the land," and referred to its gross effects on the colonized portions of this continent by the mid-eighteenth century.

From the time the white man cut his first clearing on the face of this continent, built his first fence, hung his first hawk—skyward, from the top rail of a fence—the broad balance of natural systems here became skewed. Until that time the native humans were too few in number or too satisfied with the way things were to change the picture.

Much of what our culture has inflicted has been indirect, less than obvious, insidious in nature, and has affected far more species and systems than the black bear.

But not all things wrought by modern industrial North American man have produced negative effects on the black bear. Some have been positive. Modern man, guided by his penchant to manage things and his newly rediscovered value in natural systems, has restored and improved certain aspects of the damaged wild machinery. Exactly which aspects is not easy to answer here. Nonetheless, we shall attempt to scrutinize separately a number of our influences.

Fur Trade and Bounties

As the beaver, a staple of the fur trade that catalyzed the opening of backcountry Canada and the northern U.S., began to disappear under trapping pressure, the pelt of the black bear rose in value. By the 1700s a bear hide in Massachusetts Colony was worth as much as a beaver pelt. Pressure on black bears in some areas became heavy. From two oak and chestnut bordered river valleys in West Virginia, for instance, over 8,000 bear skins were lifted in just three consecutive seasons, beginning in 1805. In a nearby valley during one of those years two men killed one

hundred and thirty-five bears in three fortnights. That's three per day for six weeks. At the same time, trading posts as far west as Wisconsin each handled up to a hundred bear hides per year.

By 1839, black bear hides were showing up in trade as far north as northern Labrador. By the mid-1800s, when the beaver was virtually extirpated east of the Mississippi and its European market value was finally failing, posts throughout the West from Vancouver to Idaho Falls were trading black bear hides. By 1887 in Lac du Flambeau, Wisconsin, the value of a bear pelt had risen to as high as eighteen dollars. A gallon of rendered bear oil cost four dollars. Several historians, Matthiessen among them, suggest that the effects of the fur trade era on populations of its trade species linger with us today.

The fur trade, as we know, was followed closely and eventually replaced by a far more dangerous habit know as agriculture. With farming and settlement came bounties. A bounty is a fee paid by the state or other unit of local government to anyone offering proof of having killed a particular animal. The particular animals in this case were predators: wolves, bears, coyotes, and so on. A pair of ears, a nose or a paw was usually required as proof that a kill had been made before a bounty fee was paid.

The concept of bounties has, as we now know, no logical justification, no biological basis. Charges against the persecuted predators were habitually inflated or erroneous, and the reduction of their populations by bounty hunters was ineffective anyway. Bounties offered only one value to the American settler: an outlet for the rancid and feckless rage he felt toward what he perceived to be his greatest competition and threat. "The presence of the black bear was second only to the approach of an Indian war party in its power to raise the early settlers to a high pitch of excitement," wrote A.W. Schorger, a natural historian of northern Wisconsin.

Despite their waste and ineffectiveness, black bear bounties remained in effect from Maine to Montana well into the twentieth century. New York was first to drop its black bear bounty in 1904,

Bountied in one state or another until 1965, the black bear is now a prized game animal in twenty-eight states.

Pennsylvania the following year. In New Hampshire, after one hundred and twenty-five years of paying bear bounties, about one hundred per year, the legislature dropped the idea in 1955. (Since 1882, nearly $100,000 in rewards had been paid out, and there were more bears in the state at the end of the regime than when it began.) Maine repealed its bear bounty in 1957, Minnesota in 1965.

Bounties and the fur trade influenced black bear populations throughout the continent throughout the nineteenth century, but they provoked their greatest effects in the mind of man, cementing the philosophies of economics and fear to the image of the black bear. And with local exceptions, neither fur trade nor bounty had nearly the impact inflicted upon our continent by the human-caused habitat change—the war which Matthiessen described.

Habitat Change

Attrition against the land. In other words, the overwhelming of the habitat. Whose habitat? Everyone's habitat. When modern man settled North America, he selected the most fertile land for his agricultural life support and then used the richest of that, the riparian floodplains, for his heaviest, most toxic, most threatening urban development. "Bear habitat now," Dr. Lynn Rogers says, "is just the crummy stuff man didn't use." We find a twofold loss here: the reduction in overall land area available for bear habitat, and the reduction in average habitat quality when the most productive land is usurped.

The first thing to go is forest cover. Nothing harder in the way of civilization than the woods, went the prevailing logic. Those "vast wastes of forest verdure," Francis Parkman called them. By 1765 the settlers of Massachusetts had begun clearing away the chestnuts and hickories and oaks in an effort to open the land to farming. Some of the wood was used for building and heat. By 1850 what had once been nine-tenths forest was one-fifth woodland. "In the physical environment that was being created

in pre-revolutionary Massachusetts, a bear would have to become invisible, not nocturnal," writes Bill Scheller in *Sanctuary* magazine. Correct on both counts: Black bears did become more nocturnal, and most of them simply disappeared. By 1880, according to educated estimates, fewer than ten bears existed there. Perhaps none.

The trend carried throughout the colonial settlement. The first settlers arrived in the Smoky Mountains in the 1790s. By 1850, all the valley bottoms were settled, the human population was growing, the logging industry was underway, and the disappearance of large, undisturbed tracts of land was wearing heavy on the bear population. By the 1920s, about the time the chestnut blight invaded what was left there, modern man had virtually eliminated the black bear from the Smoky Mountains.

Improvements followed, however. Some by default, as when the farmers left New England and the countryside grew back to forest; and some by purposeful act, like the establishment in the 1930s of Great Smoky Mountains National Park, which kept free a large tract of land on which the oak and hickory forests recovered and to which the black bear subsequently returned in number.

But many of those improvements proved to be short-lived, particularly in unprotected areas. About the time New Hampshire grew back to mostly forest, someone ushered in an era of development across the state, selling it off for second and third homes, retirement condos, and engineered resort towns, all by virtue of the state's natural beauty and wildlife. And thereby built and paved over acre after acre of natural beauty and wildlife habitat, improving roads for more and faster vehicular traffic, inviting an urbanized and displaced philosophy into the backwoods.

Because the black bear is a forest animal, timber management incurs substantial if variable effects on bear habitat. Clearcuts, for example, while removing forest cover, likely grow in two to twenty years to early successional food-producing species, thereby enhancing black bear habitat. In drier regimes, however, high soil temperatures in the

The best bear habitat has been converted to agriculture and other development. Only the most rugged and least fertile land has been left as wildlands, and most of those areas are heavily used for recreation.

openings reduce the productivity of early seral stages. "Wet meadow" understories that produce the critical spring green-up forage may dry up instead. In some areas clearcuts are still sprayed with herbicides (berry killers) to encourage coniferous regeneration. Black bears usually avoid clearcuts larger than twenty-five acres even when productive because of increased exposure to solar radiation and the reluctance of sows with cubs and other subdominant individuals to stray far from protective cover. Partial cuts that leave sections of cover and large refuge trees may be favorable to the bears, as is the protection and enhancement of oaks and other nut-producing trees in areas where they are not abundant. Black bears throughout North America den under slash piles left behind by logging operations.

Prescribed burning in cutover areas enhances berry crops. Complete fire suppression in timber stands lends to a lower percentage of openings and much hotter and more extensive fires when they do occur. As always, that management closest to the natural regime is best. Diversification of habitat types, uneven-aged mixed stands and cutting rotations that allow for mature nut-producing trees and large den trees, particularly in moist areas where dens may be flooded by winter or early spring thaws, are paradigm to good timber management for bears and for wildlife in general.

Benefits are not always obvious. Spruce budworm invades stands of firs which commonly replace clearcut spruce stands in the north country from Maine to Minnesota. One might suppose that budworm destruction of forest areas reduces bear cover: true. But Lynn Rogers points out that budworm infestations also lead to higher populations of invading insects and raspberries—foods for black bears. The balances to be wrought are not easy, always changing with time and across the geography of the continent.

Finally in this abbreviated discussion of forest practices we stumble onto the subject of roads. In addition to the public roadways already available and under constant improvement and construction,

forest managers, with our own U.S. Forest Service in the lead, are constructing new roads into the heart of our forest country for the benefit of the heavy equipment now used by the timber industry. Smaller roads, abandoned and reseeded, offer travel corridors and, as we have seen, grasses and clover as spring and fall bear foods. Larger timber roads are too expensive to plow under and remain in perpetuity.

Allan Brody's research on the effects of roads on black bears in North Carolina afforded several believable conclusions. Black bears are reluctant to cross interstates (two bears that tried and six expensive hounds in pursuit of them were killed on an interstate highway during his brief study). They will cross less heavily traveled roads. At a certain density of roads in the bush—a density level depending on many factors including the kind and severity of traffic, kind of road, kinds of activities performed by humans there, and, most importantly, local attitudes toward bears—black bears will disappear. Brody found few bears where there was more than one-half mile of improved road per square mile of forest. Roads help hunters: seventy-three percent of the bears killed by hunters in Brody's study area in 1973 were within one mile of a road. Hound-hunters often release their hounds where a bear has crossed a road, kill the fleeing bear where it crosses another road, and then cruise the roads to pick up straying hounds. This in itself is not a threat to bear populations; true, law-abiding hunters are willingly restrained by hunting regulations that avoid an excessive number of kills. But poachers, the antithesis of hunters, unrestrained by regulation, have seriously depleted bear populations. Where poachers and roads are in excess, a female bear can nowhere find a territory remote enough to allow her survival for the four to nine years she needs to reach maturity and raise her first litter. Habitat improvements rendered by timber harvest techniques can be outweighed by the increased road access to hunters and poachers. This enhanced vulnerability can be reduced by tearing up or closing forest roads after or between cuts. On the other hand, according to Rogers, roads have not been a problem in northeastern Minnesota where bears are seldom poached.

A greater problem in northeastern Minnesota is the growing number of forest homes. Rogers found that each home in his study area accounted for one bear killed as a "nuisance" each nine years, on the average. Forest homes and "nuisance" bear kills are each increasing over much of the black bear range as the human population grows older and more people build forest retirement homes and vacation homes. These homes and other human developments become particular problems in years when natural food shortages force bears to forage farther than usual. Long movements are difficult when travel corridors are cut down, paved over, fenced off, built up, and otherwise developed. Bears are shot for being attracted to garbage, gardens, dog food, bird feeders, bee hives, apple trees, livestock, farm crops, or simply passing through. In its extreme, this phenomenon is called "habitat fragmentation." Bears are confined to the fragments. When the fragments are subdivided and consumed to the point at which bears and other species can no longer exist within, the wildlife disappears. It is precisely this faunal collapse that has rendered the black bear of Florida a threatened species. The same collapse is underway and threatening in other parts of the Southeast where bays and pocosins, those little sidehill wetland thickets, fall to the saw and bulldozer, making room for new roads and developments.

The same is true in extreme form in Mexico, where severe human overpopulation pressures have spilled out of urban areas in the forms of predator control and clear cutting for short-term agricultural advantage. In most Mexican states the black bear scarcely exists. A shadow of its former population shifts around in the remaining high-country forest cover. There is no money for wildlife research or protective management in Mexico.

Only Canada, Alaska, and a few of our northern tier of states contain vast areas of forested black bear habitat unthreatened by the builders of roads and pourers of concrete. Wild and undis-turbed, this habitat doesn't hold an acorn to the quality of what the bears once had east from the spine of the Appalachians.

Foods

Whenever man changes the forest he influences food availability for the black bear. When he raises food crops or livestock he may offer a new potential food source to the bears, but at the same time he puts himself in competition with them. Agriculture in bear country becomes little more than a baiting process, a technique of entrapment. More often than not, however, the crafty bear escapes with the alternate food—sometimes the apples, honeybee larvae, corn or sheep necessary for its survival during a poor year in a landscape high-graded by human takeover. Like most predators, the black bear is blamed for more than its share of damage.

In northeastern Minnesota, garbage can be the number one food value item in the local black bear diet when berry and hazelnut crops fail. Rogers has observed larger size, higher reproductive rate, larger litters, and earlier age of first breeding among bears which supplement their diets with garbage. Do the bears become addicted to garbage? Apparently not. He has watched them ignore a tub of beef fat and travel twenty miles to a hazelnut stand to feed. In Pennsylvania, Gary Alt told me, a bear visiting a dumpster will be live-trapped and moved only a few days walk away. By the time it returns the dumpster is empty and the bear disregards it.

What about addiction to other human-derived foods? In Idaho, when black bears and sheep compete for succulent spring grasses, the juxtaposition of the two species may lead to predation on sheep, and thereafter to the killing of bears by the sheep herders. Researchers there noted that while some bears showed specific interest in the muttons, many bears avoided them, and none left their home ranges to follow the flock.

Bears are intelligent, hungry animals with superior noses and one-track minds. They need not

subsistence crimes are concentrated today in our cities. Not many bears in that habitat. Nonetheless, bear poaching is a growing industry, particularly in the West, from Arizona and California north to British Columbia and Saskatchewan.

"It would boggle your mind to know how much is going on," an undercover fish and game agent told me recently. He had been visiting bars in Idaho, looking for trouble, so to speak. "Before you and I could drink a six-pack," he said, "we both could have an illegal hunt lined up."

Why poach black bears when many states offer two seasons and the opportunity to bait them? Forgot to buy a permit, perhaps? Not time to wait for the season? Don't believe in game laws? Too many black bears anyway? All likely excuses, according to fish and game wardens I've talked to. But the modern poaching network thrives on the value of contraband extracted from the carcasses of black bears.

Black bear parts have long held some worth. In 1867, when it was perfectly legal to do so, John Perry of Algoma, Wisconsin, killed a bear and later sold the hide for ten dollars. He also sold eight gallons of pure bear oil (rendered, clarified bear fat) for sixty-four dollars and two gallons of crude oil for six, thus clearing a tidy gross profit of eighty dollars for his work. He left the meat in the woods.

There is bigger money to be made in bear parts today. The raw skin will sell for one hundred to one hundred and fifty dollars, the skull for thirty, teeth for ten, claws for a dollar or two each, and paws for up to twenty dollars each. And these are the wholesale prices paid to the supplier. Retail may be many times that. Hearts, blood and livers have a value too, making the whole bear carcass a commodity. But the big money today is in bear gall bladders. Worth up to fifty dollars each to the first middleman, a large black bear gall (they're largest in the spring) may go for up to $3,000 in South Korea, the usual site for retail sales. The going rate is sixteen dollars per gram there, and the trade is legal and abundant in shops, clinics, and hospitals throughout the country. Why South Korea? Because traditional

oriental *hanyuk* medicine still thrives there, with its component belief in the curative powers of bear gall bladder, which is taken more as a general health stimulant than as an aphrodisiac. A pinch in the tea, the traditional Korean believes, will cure indigestion, inflammation, aging, and purify the blood. Two-thirds of the value of the bear lies in the gall bladder. "We took down one old boy that was doing $20,000 to $30,000 per year, just in the gall," my contact told me.

Bear paws, served almost exclusively in Chinese restaurants, are the second most valuable contraband. Though few establishments in China offer the cuisine, many Chinese restaurants in Japan do, and since the mid-1970s the dishes have come into demand there and among orientals in the U.S.

The original and preferred source for both galls and paws is the Asiatic black bear (*Selenarctos thibetanus*), which became endangered in the 1980s due to the bear market. The carcass of a single member of this species sold for $18,500 in Korea in 1982. The following year one gall alone brought $55,000. Now the orientals prefer any wild black bear to a captive-raised Asiatic. Secondary sources in the U.S. and Canada began to grow with the booming market. What game officers term an insatiable demand for bear products has made the sale of parts of legally killed bears in America a lucrative if illegal business.

Most American contraband enters the Oriental network through Los Angeles or San Francisco en route to Japan or directly to South Korea, where its value quintuples. Much of the U.S. and Canadian trade currently filters through Idaho, where smugglers "launder" the parts under Idaho game laws that allow the purchase and sale of these parts and do not require the meat to be salvaged from a legally killed bear. The business network extends around the globe. When my friend busted the gall trader last winter in a storefront set-up, he searched the man's Cadillac out front and found eleven white rhinoceros horns with a street value in price per gram equal to that of cocaine.

How bad is the poaching problem? Worse

than most people thought. Jerry Thiessen, a bureau chief of Idaho Fish and Game, said that poaching is the most serious problem facing black bear management there. The black market harvest in California equalled at least the legal hunter kill in the early 1980s. In Great Smoky Mountain National Park, where larger bears remain inside the boundaries, due to their protection from hunting there, poachers trap bears for later release in front of "guided" dudes (the sport here lies in not getting caught). Poachers are taking a quarter of the black bears in the Shenandoah Valley, where local poachers also know the value of contraband bear parts.

A small army of undercover fish and game agents continues to secure illegal hunts, purchase contraband from bands of poachers, search the Chinese restaurants of California for stockpiles of illegally taken bear paws, and investigate Oriental herb shops—there are three hundred in Los Angeles alone—for those dear little vials of powdered gall. In 1981, California agents busted a small ring of bear poachers. In 1987 and 1988, bear poachers and black marketing rings were busted in Arizona, Virginia, and New England. But the agents invariably tell us the more they bust, the more they find. All over the continent people kill bears for profit, often taking only a small, bitter organ from under the left lobe of the liver. And maybe the paws, if they feel they have time . . . and leave the rest to rot. In the most blatant cases, perhaps increasing now due to preference in the Korean market, whole bears, ungutted, are lugged to the freezer for eventual payoff and export.

Research

We cannot fairly cover the subject of human influence without mentioning the possible effects on black bears incurred by the researchers themselves. Drugs used to immobilize the bears may have an effect on the bears' mental processes and long-term behavior. Biologist today are using milder anesthetic options, often with ready antidotes and wide parameters of ursine tolerance.

How do these drugs affect the bears? In a recent symposium on the subject, wildlife biologists found no significant relationship between the administration of drugs and bear aggression toward humans. Regarding the effect of the mixture of drugs in current use, we can refer to a single test case in which a biologist accidentally fired a dart into his own leg. He was loaded for small bear at the time. He grew immediately tired and depended on his associates to carry him off the mountain. He awoke hours later in a hospital bed, recovered fully, and has suffered no flashbacks.

Baiting to traps or for observation may cause changes in feeding patterns, often enhancing the bears' diets. Use of traps rarely causes injury, but the possibility is there and depends upon the care and knowledge of the individual trapper. One biologist I talked to hypothesized that certain frequently retrapped study animals may begin to associate easy food with unnatural containers, such as garbage cans, dumpsters and even tents, similar to culvert traps. We were talking about grizzlies at the time, and I thought of Lynn Rogers' statement about how bears are intelligent and perpetually hungry and are bound to know good food by the odors alone, without any learned association. In most cases, any of these effects are minor if present at all, and involve a tiny fraction of the black bears on the continent.

Even the radio collars bolted around their necks appear to bother the bears little. On a recent mission in the Minnesota bush, Rogers and Wilker pulled a collar over the head of an immobilized study bear without opening it—she could have shed it anytime during the year. Gary Alt once observed one of his subjects in the act of breeding within hours of receiving her collar.

Management

Left alone, black bears are entirely capable of managing themselves. They disperse to optimum

densities, find and recycle the proper foods, conserve their habitat, police their ranges and territories, and reckon with nuisance members of their own population and others. Management "needs," as we tend to call them, arise when either the bears become too much of a nuisance to humans, or vice versa. The general goal of black bear management is the maintenance of populations of bears within logical parameters while discouraging and removing nuisance behaviors.

Nuisance black bear behavior generally involves males, the wider-ranging gender and also the one which disperses cross-country in the sub-adult stage. Eighty to ninety percent of nuisance bears trapped in studies across North America are males. Nuisance behavior occurs most frequently when natural food concentrations are unavailable. Bears are sensitive and intelligent and quick to turn to human foods when available, and therefore fast to become nuisances—some of them, anyway—when the potential exists. More than sixty-five percent of all wildlife-people conflicts in British Columbia involve black bears. Even in the Yukon, black bears become nuisances where garbage is available near human habitation.

What exactly is nuisance behavior? It is difficult to define. To some people, any bear bold enough to peer through the shrubbery at woods edge is a terrible nuisance. But real nuisance behavior generally exhibits itself through either close proximity to humans or actual damage, from spilled garbage cans to ruined beehives to ravaged livestock. Aggression toward humans is usually considered a nuisance, even when human behavior precipitates the incident. Aggressive behavior ranges from the charge at a camper's food by a habituated or just hungry bear (usually mistaken as a charge toward the camper himself) to the extremely rare and unlikely attack by a predaceous bear, which usually ends in the execution of the offending animal.

Other forms of nuisance may be dealt with in gentler fashion, although in most corners of the continent any bear depredating crops or livestock is usually considered fair game for the farmer. And whenever crop damage occurs, any bear is a depredating bear. More of a one-sided feud between the species than a management plan, this is what happens when politics outspeaks biology. In New Hampshire, for example, for a decade ending not long ago the legislature held a law requiring the fish and game department to kill any bear trapped near the site of a depredation. Until the law was repealed, a retired game officer recently told me, grinning with subversion, the field crews had terrible luck in trapping the culprits.

Depredating bears are still shot or shot at—"A little lead goes a long way in a bear training program," a Wyoming outfitter reported—but other measures can be taken. Honey laced with a sickening agent such as lithium chloride has been placed in front of bee hives in an attempt to condition bears not to desire honey. Gary Alt, in his interminable quest to see bears and humans live together within the confines of a fertile and crowded Pennsylvania, has published techniques for effective electric fencing and the use of ten-foot-tall bear-proof platforms for hives. Watchdogs, he says, may help too. Bear managers in the West are suggesting that sheepherders avoid the lushest meadows for a few weeks in early spring when the bears need them most, and thus avoid the likelihood of bear-sheep interactions.

In both front-country and backcountry camping areas, bear nuisance behavior is usually encouraged by overt feeding or careless storage of human food and garbage. In a recent Yosemite study, ninety-two percent of the campers questioned by researchers stated that they had stored their food properly, but on-site checks demonstrated that only three percent actually had. Proper food storage in campsites with high bear-visitation now may include the use of permanently installed bear-proof lockers and lightweight plastic food canisters. In the front-country, bear-proof garbage cans with openings resembling those of pull-down mailboxes remove the food rewards of black bears that lurk in camping

Garbage enables black bears to grow and reproduce more rapidly, but lures them into places where they are killed by irate or fearful landowners. Where bears and campers mix, there are plenty of opportunities for bears to get in trouble if food is available. Many wilderness recreation areas now have fifty to one hundred times more people in summer than when people lived off the land. Habituated, campground-raiding black bears are a product of an unnatural number of people making an unnatural amount of food available to the bears.

areas. Aversive conditioning including wax and rubber bullets, sound blasts, and mildly noxious solutions in backpack "baits" have been used with some success. Some behaviorists even suggest that humans in black bear habitat might better learn what human behaviors deter and turn away bears without decreasing human safety, in order to reduce the food reward of a bear-human encounter. As always, public education is a critical need.

Then we have the suggestion that alternate human food offerings, placed correctly, might keep bears away from campsites. Used temporarily in the worst years of natural food failures and bear nuisance problems, the technique has shown promise. The bears shifted from the campsites to the feeding areas, and then abandoned both when natural foods became more abundant again. When one biologist first related this idea to me, I acknowledged that it seemed biologically feasible, but philosophically off-base for national park or wilderness area use. Far better, I thought, to re-establish natural food concentrations than to offer unnatural supplies. After all, the natural systems are what the parks are supposed to encourage. Maybe so, he said, but millions of humans hiking through the back country each year with their little tents and tempting freeze-dried food packets aren't very natural either.

The relocation of problem bears to areas of low human density represents another popular management tool for riddance of nuisance bears. It should be accompanied by the removal or correction of conditions that lured the bear in the first place. Translocated black bears have been known to return from as far away as one hundred and forty-two straight-line miles to trapping sites.

Take a bear more than forty to seventy-five air miles away from the site where he committed his nuisance, however, and he is usually less likely to return, particularly if it's a typical nuisance bear—a ranging subadult male. Or, as Alt has suggested, move the bear just far enough away so that by the time it does return in a week or two the lure has been removed and all remains quiet. Not only time saving, economic and efficient, Alt's technique tends not to confuse the social network at either end of the translocation.

In extreme cases of extirpation, black bears have been reintroduced to former ranges. Between 1959 and 1968, three hundred black bears from Manitoba and Minnesota were released into their old and empty niche in the northern and western forests of Arkansas. By 1970 the number of bear sightings increased, and by 1978, biologists estimated a population of more than 1,000 black bears there. Today, Arkansas' bear populations support a hunt.

Between 1964 and 1967 a similar release of one hundred and fifty-six Minnesota bears occurred in Louisiana. Some of the bears wandered into neighboring states; no hunt has yet been established there. California biologists moved black bears into the mountains in the southern portion of that state. If this transplant was successful, it is now threatened by the high level of poaching throughout the area.

By 1990 black bears were hunted in twenty-eight states and throughout forested Canada except on Prince Edward Island and Newfoundland. Licensed hunting is the most controllable source of attrition to black bear populations and therefore one of the most important management tools. The primary management need in Pennsylvania, Alt told me, is the control of hunter pressure. Bear hunting seasons can be shortened, cut for a year or more, or subjected to a quota system to control the number of bears killed. Biologists go further than that, however, shrewdly scheduling seasons to protect the productive and critical adult-sow segment of bear populations. By establishing separate hunting seasons for black bears, instead of allowing hunters to shoot then incidentally during concurrent deer hunting seasons, hunters become more discriminating and selective of the bears they shoot. That is, they wait for larger quarry, bigger bears that are more likely to be males. Since pregnant sows usually den earlier than other bears, and females usually den before males, a season set to begin after

the onset of female denning will also protect the productive segment of bear populations.

While negative sentiment often arises over hunting black bears over bait and with dogs (techniques accepted more in areas of thick forest cover, some of it considered impenetrable to the average hunter), both techniques result in greater hunter selectivity and the killing of larger bears, mostly males, again protecting the sows to some extent. The use of radiotelemmetry on bear hounds results in, at most, slightly greater hunter success, according to a recent study in Vermont.

Habitat management, always a key tool in wildlife management, holds great importance here as well. Preservation of mature oak stands one hundred years old and older, encouragement of berries and other soft mast, protection of den trees—particularly south of Pennsylvania where winter thaws may flood earth dens—and perhaps even the replacement of the American chestnut will all improve habitat for black bears. So will restricting the sizes of clearcuts, controlled burning for the production of soft mast, encouragement of hard mast production by a variety of oaks and other mast species (ash, beech, gum, dogwoods, grape) across a variety of ecological sites, promotion of a variety of alternate soft masts as well, and encouragement of whitebark pine production in the Rockies.

But more important in many areas, particularly in the beleaguered East, is the protection of forested land from further development. In Florida, where habitat fragmentation busted the bears into endangered status, biologists tell us that a critical minimum area for useful black bear habitat is now more a function of the surrounding land-use patterns than of the area's actual habitat quality. In other words, bear habitat in Florida is now the exception and not the rule.

All this clamor about poaching levels and critical habitat sounds more like management of a threatened species, not of a game species. And with good reason. After all, the black bear is threatened in some parts of its range, and completely extirpated

from others. While the black bear is numerous and productive elsewhere, its low reproductive rate, slow recolonization ability, and the difficulty in assessing its actual population trends all combine to make it possible for local populations of black bears to greatly diminish without obvious warning. Once in remission, bear populations require much attention and long periods of time to regain both territory and density again.

De facto wilderness in the East provides the only stability "in a system where instability may have extirpated the species," writes Michael Pelton, an eminent black bear research biologist working in the southern Appalachians. "Wilderness," he notes, "remains at the core of the species' needs."

Wilderness? Large chunks of undeveloped, unbroken land, at least. Whatever is left. Whatever might be saved.

In critical situations, managers have established sanctuaries, which they believe may be a viable alternative to closure of hunting seasons in areas with declining bear populations. Sanctuaries are areas protected from hunting and road building so that less-mobile female bears may reproduce successfully and "restock" surrounding habitat (preferably national or state parks, forests, or wildlife refuges guaranteed to be undeveloped). Minimum refuge size depends upon local bear home range sizes and must include complete ecological units containing everything the bears need. Biologists have recommended refuges no smaller than 10,000 acres in the Southeast and 25,000 acres in Pennsylvania. Pisgah Bear Sanctuary in North Carolina, as an example, contained ninety percent of resident bears' fall home ranges within its 55,000 acres, but still suffered a high mortality rate. Poachers appear to be the major problem. While the sanctuary is large enough to ensure at least a remnant population and protect a breeding nucleus, it may not function to those ends if enforcement of wildlife laws doesn't curtail the poachers' activities. As usual, as always, wildlife management on this continent depends

Black bears need large, unbroken areas of forest for habitat. Forest fragmentation—the conversion of forests to smaller, isolated sections of habitat—throughout the bears' range will ultimately be the species limiting factor.

finally on people management. And the management of any species must involve both behavior and numbers.

Human Attitudes, the Present, the Future

When it comes to bears, any bears, humans tend to act out of fear until convinced otherwise. And that takes a long time, but it is coming. An age of enlightenment about black bears has nearly materialized. The same human nature that has reacted with almost automatic fear at the presence of a black bear is beginning to react with understanding, even affinity. For example: In the Catskill Mountains of New York, where the bear population had sharply declined by the 1970s, a study of public attitudes showed that a majority of private landowners, corporations, even camp managers missed the bears. Most, including half those who had experienced bear problems in the past, favored rebuilding the population.

Even more powerful are the comments recently solicited from visitors who suffered injury or property damage from the bears of Great Smoky Mountain National Park. (Among the visitors, fewer than one in a million was injured. Virtually all injury occurred while the "victim" fed or approached bears.) Nearly half of those answering admitted fault in the predicaments. Two-thirds said the bears were no major threat, and over ninety percent had already returned to the park or planned to. Speaking of the bears, one camper commented, "They were here first. We are the intruders."

"It's a people problem rather than a bear problem," wrote another.

"Man is the intruder, as usual."

"The damage we sustained was slight and well deserved."

Among those sustaining bodily injury: "I don't think it would be right to punish a bear for being curious."

"The bear could hardly be blamed for using his instincts."

In pausing to think, we mirror the black bear's tolerance of our own species, and we signal, I think, the beginning of a truer understanding of the black bear.

"Human attitudes toward the bears are continually improving," Gary Alt wrote recently. Why? Modern enlightenment, the environmental renaissance we continue to struggle through here in North America, plays a key role. But I believe there is more to the picture. "People desperately need bears and bear stories," writes Ted Williams. On a continent on which half a million black bears still make their living and over three hundred million humans lurk about, we need our fellow species now more than ever. If for no other reason than to maintain our strained camaraderie—a two-million-year-old relationship based on the close association of two curious, intelligent, wide-ranging, fully adaptable and potentially powerful omnivores.

Somewhere along the line the quality of that relationship fell away. That people rush to see bears, treasure their bear stories, purchase books about them and continue to find their images in the stars all evidences the need and desire to experience the old relationship, to feel the old feelings that might, in larger perspective, be called harmony.

The black bear is presently abundant in most parts of its remaining range and produces a surplus in good habitat. But bear habitat is slowly, insidiously degraded by human encroachment. The black bear, a Montana biologist told me, may be the only species of big game that has suffered a reduction in population in the U.S. in the last two decades.

Yet the black bear's future remains bright. "The black bear has demonstrated an incredible ability to adapt to human encroachment if some escape cover is maintained," writes Gary Alt. "I am very optimistic about the future of this animal."

Black bears are normally day-active, retiring an hour or two after sunset and awakening about a half hour before sunrise. However, bears that feed in campgrounds or residential areas may become nocturnal to avoid people.

CHAPTER 10

THE PILGRIMAGE

Beneath a gray sky, a large and frozen lake, an intricate pattern of birches along the horizon, against a land white with snow. A desolate, beautiful, deserted scene. Almost deserted: Along one shore a band of humans, dressed for the cold, drifted in single file down the lake. These people belonged to a primitive, struggling culture that had recently, in geologic perspective, invaded this edge of the boreal forest. The previous evening they had shared a feast, clan-fashion, in preparation and celebration. An elder had spoken in solemn tones, reminding the others of the significance of their quest.

Two scouts led them this morning. They trod down the lake, turned eastward through the shoreline birches, and proceeded into the bush along a blazed trail. The scouts had followed a bear in these woods late the previous autumn and marked its den to be located now, during the bear's defenseless winter sleep. The crusted snow gave way repeatedly under their feet. The trail seemed long, but they were hardy people—and hungry too—and they persevered.

In a boulder-studded tract of the forest lined with alder and spruce thickets and overseen by huge white pines, the procession halted. The people gathered. The scouts signaled that the den was nearby and selected the proper site for the fire—for warmth as well as spiritual reasons. One was kindled, emblazoned with fuel. Smoke rose into the low sky. No wolf howled, no raven croaked. Only the fire spoke.

In quiet reverence now the people filed to the den. The scout who had found it unwrapped his cloak and spread it like a prayer blanket before the chamber's buried entrance. One by one each pilgrim approached, knelt, and bowed his or her head toward the bear mother under her rock. Each man, each woman, each child appeared to meditate for a moment there. Then they regrouped. The presence of the bear and the voices of her cubs inspired optimism, gaiety, laughter.

The elder raised a hand and the gathering

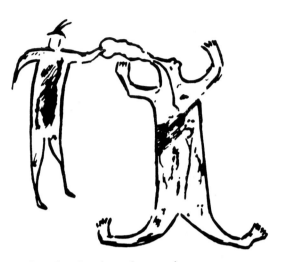

Bear drawing, from photograph
Courtesy of *American Indian Art Magazine*

The actual petroglyph was carved into a sandstone cliff in Dakota County, Nebraska, but the date and maker are not known. It may illustrate an Indian receiving supernatural power from a bear.

quieted. He delivered his litany while a scout excavated the entrance with a wooden snowshoe. The elder, secure in his dogma and unafraid, lowered his torso and squinted into the subterranean darkness of the rock crevice. Tension mounted among the tribe. Then with a flourish he thrust a sharp five-foot spear, a special and carefully crafted instrument, into the void, into the flesh of the bear mother. . . . He withdrew the spear, stood, and studied the blood at its tip.

The she-bear, unable to rouse quickly enough from her lethargy, was subdued. The elder spoke to her, calling her by name, and apologized. From the hole the scouts extracted two small cubs and passed them among the human gathering, which showed great delight. Then the female's body was dragged out, not onto snow but onto the blanket. The elder treated her with reverence. He held her paw, felt her backbone to measure her fat, and carefully turned her lower lip—big medicine among the Woodland

On following pages: A hypodermic syringe attached to the end of a "jab stick" is used to inject a sedative into the sleeping adult.

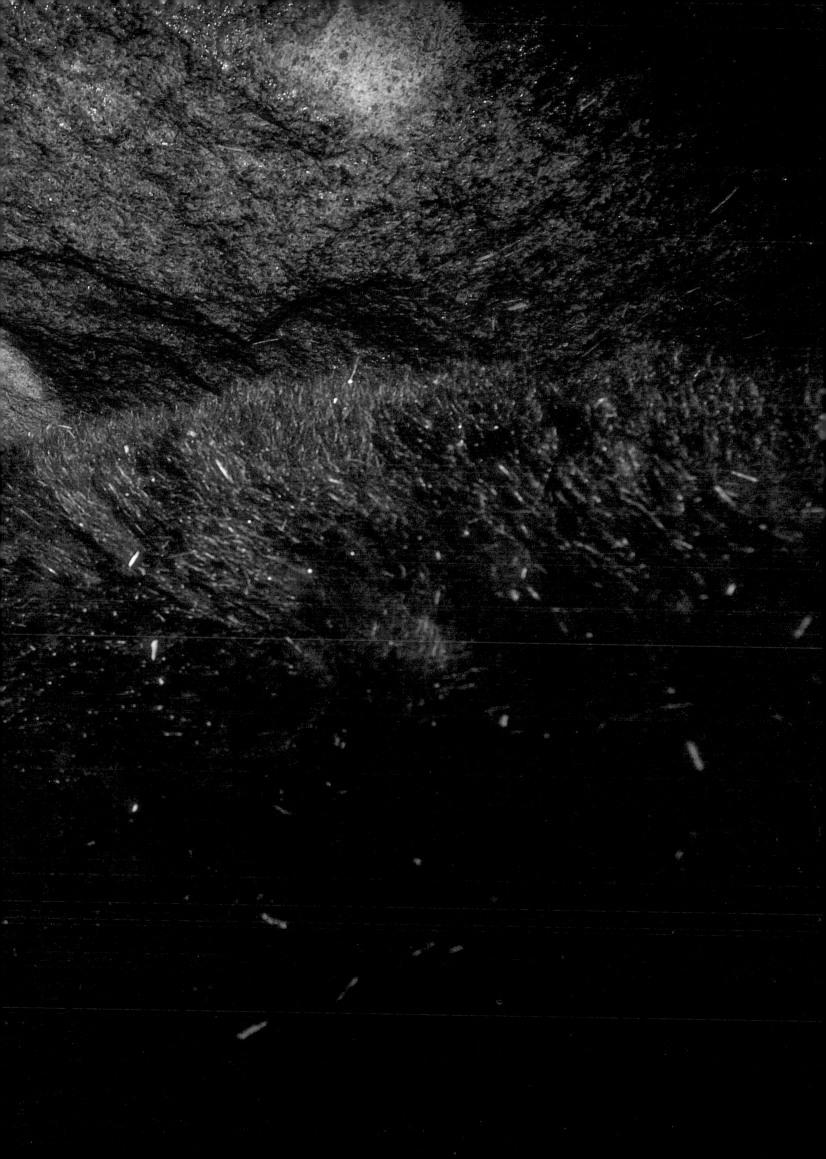

Cree. One by one the celebrants touched the bear. Her four paws were bound with rope to a carrying stick, which the scouts shouldered, raising her limp carcass there before the den in which she had intended to pass the winter. A long pink tongue spilled out to one side of her jaws. Various members of the band wandered back to squat by the fire. Now the real work would begin.

Is the Bear Cult dead? You won't convince me of it. And I should know; I've observed the ceremony myself. The account I describe in detail above occurred on March 26, 1988, and I took part as witness and celebrant.

This was no anomaly. Similar rituals occur quite often today. Our little band was comprised largely of local environmental group members with common interests. We were poking around in Kawishiwi country again, not far from Ely, Minnesota. The elder, of course, was Dr. Lynn Rogers; he spoke about his work the evening before where we had dinner at the Bear Island Resort. The scouts were Greg Wilker and another field assistant. The trek was one of Roger's regular late-winter forays to renew the collar, count the cubs, and check on the general condition of a study bear. Patch played the role of the bear.

The prayer blanket was Wilker's parka. He threw it down in the spirit of chivalry for a young woman who wished to listen at the breathing hole. The remaining attendees instinctively took their turns, one by one, listening to the cubs chuckle, and bowing low to sample the gentle musk laced with the fragrance of warm moss rising from the opening. Rogers' spear was his jab stick, its point a syringe loaded with a tranquilizing drug. He checked the needle upon withdrawal for the drop of blood that indicates an intramuscular injection. Rogers inspected Patch's paws for the shedding of the pads (nearly complete) and turned down her lip to check the identifying tattoo. To weigh the bear, Greg tied her feet to a pole-mounted scale with a soft rope. The work that followed included a variety of measurements, a collar exchange, the extraction of a blood sample (Rogers wanted to monitor her biochemistry; she appeared quite thin), and finally the repacking of bear mother and cubs into their original positions in the den and replacement of snow cover at the entrance.

The fire was indeed for warmth and spirit. The reverence and joy and wonder felt in the hearts and minds of the pilgrims was timeless.

So the Bear Cult is still alive? Of course it is. It has not disappeared but merely changed. And from the perspective of the raven overseeing things from his snag above the bush, not by much.

I am happy to report that on the trail to the den with Rogers that March day I thought little of how this research might dissolve gallstones, alleviate diabetic symptoms, treat insomnia, facilitate space travel, or even benefit the black bear itself. I was simply going out to see the creature up close one more time, maybe look her in the eyes, perhaps learn something unspeakable. My fellow travelers, I must assume, had similar goals. That is the base and basis of the Bear Cult today, and of it there is little more to be said.

We sense an image of ourselves—of our past—in the black bear, a comparative reality with similarities of physique and physiognomy, of opportunism, omnivory, bipedalism, adaptability. Separate, but related. Incontrovertibly different, though similar.

Where Leopold once saw the fierce green fire in the dying wolf's eyes we can look into the eyes of the black bear more closely and see it—alive. What we see is almost comprehensible. But not quite. We are, after all, just beginning to learn about our world again, the second time around. Poised between a past we cannot afford to lose and a mountain of impending truth, we find ourselves in another type of Kawishiwi country—this no place between—by a rapid river flowing across the broad and factual continent or our intelligence. Searching for our bearings. Circling overhead, in a stellar performance mocking our own lives, the great sky bear stalks her infinite territory, followed forever by a single cub who carries true north in the tip of his tail.

Dr. Lynn Rogers leads a modern-day "bear cult" to the den of one of his sleeping subjects in the forest of northeastern Minnesota. After locating the den and prior to removing its occupants, Rogers explains to the onlookers the procedures he and his assistant will follow in drugging and extracting the sow and her cubs. Rogers holds the cubs as his assistants remove the mother bear from the den. The smile on his face shows what many of the researcher's friends and associates already know—beyond his scientific objectivity, "the bearman" has a special fondness for his subjects.